Understanding
English Place-Names

To the memory of P. H. Reaney

who encouraged me to believe that although

I might never find the right answers I might one day become

capable of asking the right questions

UNDERSTANDING ENGLISH PLACE-NAMES

SIR WILLIAM ADDISON

B. T. BATSFORD LTD
LONDON

First published 1978

© Sir William Addison 1978

Printed in Great Britain
by J. W. Arrowsmith Ltd, Bristol
for the publishers B. T. Batsford Ltd,
4 Fitzhardinge Street, London W1H 0AH
ISBN 0 7134 0295 4

Contents

List of Illustrations

(Between pages 80 and 81)

Acknowledgements

The illustrations are by Kenneth Scowen, F.I.I.P., F.R.P.S., with the exception of no. 4 which is by Leonard & Marjorie Gayton, nos 10 and 21 which are by the late Noel Habgood, no. 19 which is by Richard Hawken, and no. 20 which is by the late Edwin Smith.

'Mark! how all things swerve

From their known course, or vanish like a dream;

Another language speaks from coast to coast;

Only perchance some melancholy stream

And some indignant hills old names preserve,

When laws, and creeds, and people all are lost.'

WILLIAM WORDSWORTH

Introduction

'History isn't something that is dead and done with; it is something that is alive and all around us . . . in things we see before our eyes.'

A. L. ROWSE

When we say that we can't for the life of us remember the name of a person or place, it is usually suggested that we are showing signs of senility. In fact, we may merely be disclosing that the name never meant much to us anyway. As General Smuts said, 'Nothing is seen when the viewer does not know what he is looking at'. Yet both personal-names and place-names were originally introduced as aids to identification and fall into similar groups. Just as a personal name ending in 'son' linked the original holder with his father, a name ending in 'ton' may link the settlement with the man who first fenced it in or dug the first ditch; but we say 'may' when we come to places because we are much more likely to go wrong in applying this basic principle to these than to persons. The first Wilson was almost certainly Will's or William's son, the first Wilmington almost certainly the 'ton' of William's (Wilhelm's) people. It does not, however, follow that all the Wiltons were Will's or William's 'tons'. The first syllable may come from wild or waste; it may come from 'well', as at Wilton in Somerset, which has a famous well dedicated to St George; it may indicate that willows once grew where the villagers now grow cabbages or graze their cattle. Wilton in Wiltshire, incidentally, means none of these. It is the 'ton' on the Wylye, the river that gave its name to the shire, which in turn was the shire that depended on the town of Wilton. So the ancestry of place-names may be as complicated as the tale of the cow with the crumpled horn.

Some place-names, like personal-names, preserve the memory of local trades or crafts. There is a Sapperton, 'village of soap-makers,' in at least four counties. Iron Acton in Gloucestershire, Cole Orton in Leicestershire and Glass Houghton in West Yorkshire are all examples of craft names. The total number of such names, however, is small. Persons rather than places are associated with crafts, whereas the number of descriptive place-names is very large indeed. The one thing that can be said about all place-names is that for one reason or another they provide clues to the character of the original settlement and to the cross-country progress of the settlers. So local historians still find the earliest recorded place-name a safe starting point for the study of their town or village. The point to note is the importance of starting with the first documentary evidence available; the name appearing there will probably bear little resemblance to the name appearing on the local Post Office.

There are many reasons for this. The original name may have been derived from a foreign word no longer in use in England. The amateur historian may never have heard it. To the expert, however, while the earliest recorded name is the only safe starting point, every modification of it provides a clue to the development of the settlement. Dialect modifications are exceptionally revealing, particularly when they combine a British name with that of an invader. The most obvious are those incorporating Norman family names. In 1154 Norman noblemen owned one thousand English castles and the religious houses were occupied by French monks of one order or another. But these are less interesting than earlier combinations which may show the persistence of the tribe that was established in the region when the Saxons or the Danes invaded. These, in turn, may show that the district was already capable of supporting a population by agriculture, whereas in regions where the older names seem to have disappeared the explanation may be that the earlier settlement was sparse; but alternatively may be that the people living there got their food by hunting and fishing and could move away when the invaders came. This will be seen when we look at the Fens, or the Somerset Levels, and discuss the persistence of Celtic types in the Pennines and elsewhere.

The intelligent traveller through place-names has the publications of the Place Name Society to guide him through the counties, and Professor Ekwall's *Oxford Dictionary of English Place Names* for making comparisons on a national scale. Professor Kenneth Cameron's *English Place-Names* is a valuable students' guide to their scientific examination. Eminent scholars have dealt with specific aspects of this extremely complex subject, but most of their work is too specialised for the layman. So it is hoped that the following pages may serve the more modest purpose of helping the general reader to see how much place-names can tell us about the evolution of our landscape. Now that we are all mobile, every signpost we pass prompts questions to those of us who are always on the look-out for evidence of local history. The dangers of starting out on false scents have been indicated; but so long as we are not setting up as experts ourselves, a later discovery of how wrong we were only adds to the fun. It also has advantages in that although we may never become clever enough to be sure that we have found the right answers, we may get better at asking the right questions, especially when we meet dialect modifications, which become stronger the further we travel from London. They strike the traveller forcibly on reaching two important rivers in the North, the Ribble in Lancashire and the Wharfe in Yorkshire. The explanation of the Ribble forming so marked a boundary is that when the names along its valley were formed those to the south lay in the old diocese of Lichfield, which included Derbyshire, where similar dialect origins are traceable. Lancashire as an independent shire was a twelfth-century creation. The Wharfe was a dividing line in Yorkshire – also late – for a reason that will be discussed later.

While these two divisions are not surprising, even as near London as in Hertfordshire we find that the eastern part of the county retains archaic characteristics in its place-names that are more akin to those of Essex than to those of west Hertfordshire. Again, the reasons are ecclesiastical. They are traceable to the boundary of the old bishopric of London. Hertfordshire, as an independent unit, did not exist before the tenth century. Similarly, linguistic differences in modern Northumberland can be traced to the influence of the prince-bishops of Durham, while in Gloucestershire and Worcestershire we have a region in which West Saxon influences are strong, as Celtic are near the Welsh border, particularly in Herefordshire. These, however, are for more readily discernible topographical reasons. That ecclesiastical influences were so strong in place-name modifications is not surprising when we recall that at the height of its power the Church owned one-third of the nation's land and property.

In looking for topographical reasons we start with rivers. The basic explanation of the rapidity and extent of racial infiltration in pre-Norman days is quite simply the fact that Britain is an island bountifully provided with streams and rivers. One of the first questions asked by the beginner in place-name studies is why so many rivers have the same name. Most are pre-English names that survive in present-day Welsh words and tend to be descriptive. Many contain at least one syllable that is repeated in a large number of river names. Even the complete names recur with puzzling frequency. They include the Avons, Stours, Calders, Colnes and Fromes. Still more confusing is the changing of the name of a river half way along its course. The Cam becomes the Granta, the lower part of the Pant in Essex becomes the Blackwater, the lower part of the Alde in Suffolk the Ore. On the other hand, the greatest of all, the Thames, has always borne the same name from its source to its mouth, even through the long reaches of its estuary. In many parts of the country the towns and villages along the river banks take their name from the river. In Essex, Suffolk and Norfolk few place-names are derived from river-names. On the contrary, quite often the smaller streams derive their names from places. The explanation of this is that the Anglo-Saxon colonisation was so strong and so complete that the earlier names failed to survive. No doubt these streams had Celtic names before the invaders came, and this supposition leads us to suspect that many places had earlier names that have now disappeared and may only be found in traditional minor names, such as field-names.

So we learn most about river-names by studying those in the far west, where Celtic populations would be more likely to survive, and also, as we shall see when we look at the Pennine country in the North, in mountainous country that failed to attract early settlers. Thus we find that Avon is identical with the Welsh *afon* and simply means 'river', that Wey, as we have it in Surrey and Dorset, is identical with Wye and, more obscurely, that the British *isca*, meaning water, takes various forms in such names as Axe, Exe, Usk and Wiske.

In the North of England we find the Norse settlers being similarly addicted to imaginative descriptive names in a way that we do not find in Anglo-Saxon districts. The Norse long 'a', which means river, occurs in the Greta, 'the strong river' and Brathay, 'the broad river'. We find also that rivers give names to towns, as in Ayton, 'the ton on the river'. For smaller streams, called brooks in the South, we find the name 'beck' in the North, which again occurs in such place-names as Caldbeck, 'cold brook', Beckermet, which means 'meeting of streams', Beckermonds, 'the junction of streams', and Birkbeck, 'beck where the birches grow'. There are other names for streams – 'burn' for example, but beck is mentioned first because it is a common element in place-names and means different things in different parts of the country. In Saxon country it may be a personal name, or it may indicate a beacon point used in a warning system. Nor does this exhaust its uses. In Shropshire, Herefordshire and Gloucestershire, as well as in certain places in eastern England, it is used for a small valley through which we may assume that a stream ran formerly if not now. It usually takes the form *bache*, and is found in Batchcott, Shropshire. Moving eastward we have it in Beachampton (Buckinghamshire), Debach, 'deep valley', Haselbech, 'hazel valley', Wisbech, 'the valley of the river Wissey', and it may be a better explanation of High Beach in Epping Forest than that given by either Buxton or Reaney. The greatest confusion arises when we pass from the Lake District, the true home of the becks, into County Durham, where a beck becomes a burn, yet is found in one or two place-names. There we may conclude that it is derived from the personal-name Becca.

These regional variations for natural features are of inexhaustible interest. In some parts the valleys through which the streams run are called deans, in others gills, in others again dales. Ravines become chines in Hampshire and Dorset, combes in Devon from the Welsh *cwm*. And even when we think we have all our rivers and valleys regionalised we find that Father Thames himself is a member of a much larger family than we might have suspected. The name is derived from a word meaning 'dark water' that is found in several Tames. Tavy in Devonshire, Taff in Wales, and even Team as far north as County Durham. And if we are surprised at the distances which separate these, what shall we say when we discover that the Devonshire Dart is identical with the Cumbrian Derwent, 'the river besides which oaks are numerous'? All we can do is agree with Sir Francis Palgrave when he said 'Mountains and rivers still murmur the voices of nations long denationalised or extirpated.'

Away from the navigable rivers, ridgeways were the most important lines of communication when place-names were being established. These ancient trackways provide clues to many of our earliest settlements. The -burys along these routes frequently mark Iron Age camps that are outside the scope of this survey except in so far as they are related to towns and villages that sprang up near them. In the South the element 'bury' may indicate a prehistoric site, as it does in Ashbury in Berkshire, Avebury and Tisbury in Wiltshire. Such earthworks as those at Harborough Banks in Warwickshire, Arbury Hill Camp in Northamptonshire, Yarborough Camp in Lincolnshire, are subjects for experts. One such, Arbour Low in Derbyshire, was a Bronze Age sanctuary. But the Iron Age camps do frequently indicate ancient trade routes that resulted in the establishment of towns along their courses. It was unusual for these defensive sites in themselves to be capable of providing the minimum needs of even a small population. They rarely, for example, had a water supply. So we conclude that in many places a defensive site might be fortified after the original settlement had been founded. In a few places the two could grow up together. There would be no shortage of water at Glastonbury, for example, which was an Iron Age lake-village. In such counties as Cornwall, where population remained sparse, the combination of the town and the defensive works might remain combined for a long time.

As with stream-names, early names related to 'bury' are a tricky subject. Brough with a defensive meaning occurs in Derbyshire, and in both East and West Yorkshire. This might appear to be the common element in the many Broughtons found in various parts of the country. In fact, only one of the four in Lancashire is near a fortified site, the others are near brooks and find their origin in that. Broughton in Hampshire is near a barrow. Danbury in Essex, which has been said to mean 'dwellers in the woodland pasture', a delightfully appropriate derivation having regard to the many copses and spinneys in the neighbourhood, may very well have had a defensive origin.

The commonest suffixes for defended sites, of course, are the -chesters and -casters. Many are prefixed by older personal-names, such as Anna in Ancaster, Cissi in Chichester, Godmund in Godmanchester, all of which are Old English names. Many are plainly Celtic. As so many of these -chesters are associated with the Roman occupation it is surprising how few are of Roman origin. It is, in fact, one of the mysteries about place-names that so few of them are Roman. The first element in Dorchester is pre-English, but a large proportion of -chesters have Saxon prefixes, and in some places we can tell when we are moving from one racial kingdom to another by the change from -caster to -chester. For example, the river Nene separates Danish Northamptonshire from Saxon Huntingdonshire, so we find Chesterton on the Saxon side confronting Castor on the Danish, the two separated by a bridge formerly guarded by a Roman station. With both the -casters and the -chesters we find curious elisions resulting in such pronunciations as Leicester (Le'ster), Bicester (Bi'ster), Worcester (Wor'ster), Gloucester (Glos'ter) and Cirencester (Si's'ter). The rot, we are assured, started with the Normans, who had difficulty in pronouncing the 'ch'.

As so many of the -burys and barrows were prehistoric, they lead us into another broad division in place-names, that between pagan and Christian, and it is a curious fact that as England is so proud of its Christian tradition hardly any of its names beginning with 'God' represent the Christian Deity. Godstow in Oxfordshire is the only one that definitely refers to the Christian god, and that is late. It did not exist until the founding of a nunnery there, which was consecrated in 1138. Some names containing 'God' are from Godwin, but there is a possibility that as there are at least six examples of Godshill, or Gadshill, and hills were frequently associated with pagan worship, 'God' may have been introduced into the name as a means of exorcising the pagan spirit. It has also to be accepted that 'god' was used for heathen deities, as an alternative to, say, Woden. We do, however, get Christ in Christchurch, Chrishall, and Cressage in Shropshire, which means Christ's oak. Saints in place-names are common everywhere, particularly in Cornwall. The many names prefixed by Abbot, Bishop, Minster and so forth are obviously late and follow the establishment of a monastery or diocese. Other Christian influences, such as the presence of the element 'Cross', have an obvious source; but they are interesting as signifying the presence of a wayside cross and may tell us something about mission routes. Temple usually indicates a place associated with the Knights Templars. Baldock, Hertfordshire, has a more obscure connection. It is derived from the Old French form of Baghdad in commemoration of the local Templars' association with that city during the Crusades.

The main interest in mapping place-names with pagan origins is in their evidence of settlement before or after the conversion, or in some regions re-conversion, to Christianity. As we should expect, we find considerable evidence of pagan superstitions in the south-east, which was invaded early, in such names as Thunderfield, Thundridge, Thurstable, Thundersley and Thunderley, all derived from worship of the mighty Thunor.

The most persistent of these pagan survivals are associated with burial customs. In some places the burial places of the dead were the places where the moot met, presumably to give solemnity to its proceedings. Modbury in Dorset and Mutlow in Cheshire are examples. In the Danelaw the Norse word *haugr* indicates a burial mound. Harland in the North Riding of Yorkshire means 'barrow land'. The Norse *hreyse* 'raise' as we have it in Dunmail Raise, Cumberland, may refer to the cairn in which Dunmail, a tenth-century Prince of Strathclyde, is buried. The Old English *bel* may mean 'funeral pyre'. Bylaugh and Belaugh mean cremation enclosure, and Belton in Leicestershire has the same origin.

The conclusion to be drawn from a study of heathen place-names is that the permanent conversion to Christianity over most of the country was slow. Northumberland is the exception. They are rare, as we should expect, in heavily wooded areas where clearings were late; but in such fertile counties as Devon and Somerset, as well as along the Welsh border, they are common. Shacklow in Derbyshire, Shuckburgh in Warwickshire, and Shucknall in Herefordshire all derive their names from *succa* 'demon or evil spirit associated with a barrow or earthwork'. There are comparable occurrences in other counties. Dragons were also associated with barrows, as in Drakelow in Derbyshire, 'the dragon's mound', a name which occurs also in Bedfordshire and Worcestershire, each preserving the myth in which Beowulf fought the fire-breathing dragon that guarded the treasure hidden under a barrow.

Belsted, meaning 'place of fire', is found in two parishes in the eastern counties. It occurs at Broomfield in Essex and near Ipswich in Suffolk, where a pagan cemetery was found that contained both inhumation and cremation burials. At Beald Farm, near Ely, according to a twelfth-century document, a tradition of burial was associated with the site. Most impressive of all, perhaps, is the great Saxon barrow in the original churchyard at Taplow in Buckinghamshire.

Instances of the subsequent consecration of a pagan site will be given in the course of our tour of the provinces. The significance of them is that they show how seriously the bishops took Pope Gregory's instruction to Abbot Mellitus, a missionary to the pagan English, that he should not destroy the heathen temples, but adapt them to Christian use. Harrow-on-the-Hill is an example of this being done, and the fact that so many churches stand on mounds can be explained similarly. Harrow has its root in *hearg*, which means 'heathen shrine'. Even more revealing are the discoveries at Harrow Hill, near Angmering in Sussex, where a pagan religious sanctuary was excavated on an Iron Age camp. So many ox skulls were unearthed that it became clear that the earthwork must cover more than a thousand and that this was a place where cattle were slaughtered in accordance with the custom mentioned by Pope Gregory of 'sacrificing many oxen to devils'. Broxted in Essex may be so named because animals were sacrificed there. This custom is confirmed by Bede, who records that November was 'the month of blood', or sacrifice.

The counties that best repay study through place-names of this transition from paganism to Christianity are Essex, Surrey, Sussex and Staffordshire, where heathenism survived until late in the seventh century. This shows that while hills were chosen for worship by some, woods and groves were chosen by others as sacred sites. The name Easwrith, borne by a Sussex Hundred, may mean 'the thicket of the gods'. In these, pagan wells, or springs, became holy wells in which converts were baptised. The pagan god of wells was Wan. The favourite dedication of holy wells was to Anne, which suggests that the early missionaries brought their converts into the fold by persuading them that their salvation depended on Anne, not Wan. Two examples in the North of England of holy wells which probably originated in this way are Halliwell in Lancashire and Hellifield in West Yorkshire. That trees as well as wells were venerated is shown by the reference to an ash-tree 'which the ignorant call holy' mentioned in connection with the boundaries of Taunton in an ancient charter.

When we come to considering early Christian influence on place-names we find that the common element 'stow', meaning place, frequently had an ecclesiastical association. Professor Mawer found that of those he examined seventy-five *per cent* were either associated with a saint's name or with a prefix meaning holy. This, he suggested, indicated a close connection with the Welsh *llan*. Following up this line of enquiry, we find that places with the name of a saint incorporated in them provide clues to the original settlement. In Essex, for example, the strength of the persistence of lay, as distinct from clerical, manorial influence is reflected in that few church dedications are found in Essex place-names, whereas in Suffolk, where the influence of the great abbey of St. Edmundsbury was dominant, they appear frequently. Another clue to the early history of a place may be found where the dedication of the church is a saint whose festival falls on the day of the local fair. This may indicate the importance of the town as an early trading centre, particularly if it is located on an ancient pilgrim or trade route.

Most of these names deriving from ancient sites or superstitions set the imagination working in a manner that may not be entirely scientific. Happily we can be more precise about the origins of the vast majority of our place-names. They begin with those that are derived from the Old English -*ingas*, which is plural, but usually survives in the final -ing, which may appear to be singular. Most of these -ing endings have a personal name as their prefix and denote ownership by a particular man, or the place where his descendants lived; but -ingas really means 'people of', so should indicate the region where the followers of a single leader lived. These always denote the earliest Anglo-Saxon settlements and consequently are found, as we shall see, in greatest numbers in Sussex and Essex. They usually indicate settlement between AD 450 and AD 550. A few of them have a topographical first syllable, as Tooting meaning a look-out spot, or Epping and Uppingham, which mean settlements of upland dwellers. Where we find this we ask 'Why upland?' or 'Upland from where?' With Epping the answer is 'upland from Waltham Abbey', the earlier settlement. Barking in Essex means 'dwellers among the birch trees', which is now as inappropriate as Epping is appropriate.

The -hams come next in antiquity, and often have similar derivations. Buckingham, for example, is the ham of Bucca's people, Nottingham, the ham of Snot's people. In some places, Wokingham for example, we have both *ing* and *ham*. Where there is a personal name as prefix, a tribal origin with an overlord's ownership and control is indicated. Sometimes a topographical name has a link with a similar name in the country from which the invaders came, suggesting that they were at home in that kind of country. These combined elements can be fascinating. The *ir* in Irby, a name found in several counties, obviously means 'Irishman's farm'; but how do we explain the continuation of the Irish element into the Scandinavian *by*, except by assuming that the Norsemen reached the place from Ireland, so that it was originally an Irish-Norwegian settlement? In some places we find a name indicating groups of people settling in alien territory. The most remarkable of these is Flimby in Cumberland, so named from a group of Flemings who settled there during the 1100s. Other examples of this are Saxton, Saxham and Saxtead, when away from Saxon kingdoms, and Ingleby, 'village of the English', suggesting that the English were in a minority thereabouts.

Professor Mawer found the following *percentages* of hams: Norfolk twenty-six, Surrey twenty-five, Sussex twenty-one, Cambridge twenty-two, Essex twenty-one. The *percentage* falls as we go westward until along the Welsh border the figures become: Cheshire five, Staffordshire one, Shropshire one, Herefordshire three, Worcestershire five, Gloucestershire two. When we come to examine the *tons*, the commonest element in English place names, signifying an enclosed town or village, which did not develop into town until the Middle Ages, the proportions are reversed in regional distribution. Cheshire has fifty-one *per cent*, Shropshire fifty-eight, Staffordshire forty-eight, Herefordshire sixty-six, Worcestershire forty-five and Gloucestershire forty-eight, while in the east the highest concentration is in Cambridgeshire, with forty *per cent*.

The -tons are everywhere, usually prefixed with a personal name; but sometimes descriptive. The -bys occur sporadically over the greater part of England, but least frequently in the South. They follow the lines of Danish settlement. Of more than seven hundred of them recorded in Domesday, five hundred and forty-three were in the Danelaw Shires. There were two hundred and seventeen of them in Lincolnshire, only three in Suffolk. Thwaite as a suffix is practically confined to Cumbria, north Lancashire, and Yorkshire, with a few in Nottinghamshire. Topographically descriptive endings, such as -field and -hurst, came slowly as the forests were felled and the marshes drained. But all are old in historically recorded time. Most names including 'new' for example, are at least eight hundred years old.

The most commonly recurring among minor names is, surprisingly, Coldharbour (the name originally given to a wayside shelter from the weather). It is found in thirty-four counties extending from Northumberland to Cornwall. It occurs twenty times in Lincolnshire, thirty times in Kent, eighteen in Surrey, twenty-six in Sussex, and what seems especially odd is that more than half the total of three hundred and seven should be in the ten southernmost counties, while Durham, Lancashire and several Midland counties lack it altogether. Perhaps southerners might think it equally surprising that there are forty 'Mount Pleasants' in Yorkshire!

It is such apparent anomalies as these that make the study of place-names so fascinating, particularly where an unexpected racial root turns up, or a Celtic group in a region where practically every other name is Saxon or Scandinavian. One of the most puzzling of these is Walton, which may mean 'the -ton of the Britons or of the British serfs'. But it may mean a settlement in a wood, on a wold, or even by a stream. Only by looking at these confusing names in their historical and topographical context can we speculate intelligently on which origin is likely to apply. With Walton, the survival of the British is generally taken as applicable to the two in Cheshire, those in Derbyshire, one in Essex, and one near Folkestone. Walton-le-dale in Lancashire and Walton-on-the-hill in Surrey remind us how often compound names come from documents in Law Latin or Law French and are clearly extended for precise identification.

So in one way or another all these names contribute to the story of the gradually unfolding relationship between place and people, a relationship that in the early stages can most profitably be studied from the examination of natural features, such as hills and streams, and the reasons for their attraction to the people who made their homes near them. Hunters were attracted by one kind of country, shepherds by another, and agriculturalists by yet another. But it was from the Saxons that most of the names came. They raided the east and south coasts in the fourth century and in the fifth established themselves firmly in Sussex and later in Essex. By the middle of the sixth century the Jutes from Denmark and elsewhere had occupied much of Kent, the Isle of Wight and Hampshire. While from this time onwards the Angles pursued their relentless course through the Midlands, the North-east and the East to form the kingdoms of Mercia, Northumbria and East Anglia, the Saxons were steadily establishing themselves in kingdoms to which they gave as names the points of the compass. The Battle of Deorham (Gloucester) in 577 took them into the Bristol Channel, the Battle of Chester in 616 laid open the North from the Irish to the North Sea. Can we wonder that their record was to prove permanent?

Finally, before making our way through the regions, it may be helpful to have a note on their major divisions. Counties were established under Norman rule. Those with Saxon elements in their names are readily explained. They were Saxon kingdoms. The Oxford Dictionary gives as one definition of Shire: 'A term applied to other parts of England by the inhabitants of East Anglia, Kent, Sussex, Essex and Surrey'. Be that as it may, the use of the term is complicated, and one misunderstanding needs to be removed at the outset. A Shire is not, as some writers have said, a region sheared off from a Kingdom. Nor are the Shires confined to the hunting country of the Midlands. They are characteristic of the Midlands and the South as the result of the social organisation of those parts by the Danes in a manner to be described later. Hampshire was the first of the Shires adopted for this purpose. York was the first place in the North to give its name to a Shire, and when it did so the City itself was divided into six of them! So a Shire was merely an administrative district to the Yorkshiremen, which might be large or small according to convenience.

Farther North, the bishops of Durham called their 'liberties' Shires. For general purposes, however, a Shire can be defined as a jurisdiction or administrative district associated with the name of its principal town. That is what the Midland Shires are, each with its sheriff, or shire-reeve, and its shire-moot. The oldest names of county districts are Celtic. The first part of Cumberland, now revived in Cumbria, is an anglicised form of the Welsh Cymry. Kent is from *canto*, meaning rim or edge, a name as appropriate for extreme south-east as it is for the extreme south-west, where we find it again in Cornwall.

Within the county divisions are the Hundreds, usually bearing names that provide other clues to local history. They were areas designated for the support of a hundred families and consequently varied considerably in size according to the fertility of the local soil. There were originally four in Huntingdonshire, sixty-seven in Sussex. But the Hundred was not the only Shire division. Sussex had its Rapes, Kent its Lathes, while other counties had Wapentakes. Both the Lathes of Kent and the Rapes of Sussex appear to represent the provinces of the ancient kingdoms that preceded them. Lathe means 'division of land'. Wapentakes were divisions of the Danelaw. The name is now shown as Old English, but it had Scandinavian origin and denoted the symbolic brandishing of weapons in confirmation of decisions made at public meetings. In England they were originally divisions formed for defence against the Danes, with the basic requirement that each should provide one ship. This specific use of the name resulted in the Wapentakes and the Hundreds in the same regions having distinctive histories, although they were identical as systems of administration.

Such knowledge as we have of the early history of the Hundreds is derived from the records of their assemblies or moots. As these might be held at a tree, a ford, on a hill, or near such landmarks as monoliths, preaching crosses, staples or posts, or even prehistoric barrows, their names, as the names of places, come within our scope. Staple gives its name to a Hundred in Sussex and to two, Barstaple and Thurstable, in Essex. From crosses, we have Faircross in Berkshire and Norman Cross in Huntingdonshire. Ewcross (yew cross) and Buckrose (beech cross) mark Wapentake meeting places in Yorkshire, and most delightful of all the tree names, Skyrack (shire oak) at Leeds in Yorkshire, where a plaque marks the site of the oak under which the Wapentake meetings were held.

Sepulchral mounds or tumuli, which gave special solemnity to meeting-places, are found at Bassetlaw in Nottinghamshire, Betisloe in Lincolnshire, Baldslow in Sussex, and Harlow in Essex. Among other Hundreds bearing the names of eminent persons and also associated with trees are Edwinstree in Hertfordshire and Gartree in Leicestershire.

In Scandinavian-settled districts a different name appears for an assembly, and is perpetuated in the name of the Hundred it served. Thinghoe in Suffolk was the hoe where the Danish *thing*, or assembly, was held. Similar traces of Danish rule can be found all the way up the eastern coast from Dengie, 'Danes' island', in Essex to the great Danes' Dyke of Flamborough Head, where the Dickering Wapentake meeting was held. In Devon, as we should expect, Hundreds are named after ridges or tors. Wapentake divisions are now only retained in Yorkshire, Nottinghamshire, Leicestershire and the northern parts of Lincolnshire.

In Northumberland, County Durham and Westmorland the divisions are called Wards, many of them taking their names from river valleys: Glendale, Eskdale, Lonsdale, from Glen, Esk and Lune. Others take their names from castles. So in one way or another, as Thomas Hardy put it, 'every village has its idiosyncrasy, its constitution.' The clue to this, he might have added, is usually to be found in its name, which is a kind of folk signature, as indicative of its original character as the signature of an artist on a painting.

CHAPTER ONE

South East England

KENT · SUSSEX · SURREY

Kent is the obvious starting point. It was here with the account of the Roman invasions that our recorded history began, and the three counties of Kent, Sussex and Surrey are a compact group to be studied together. Topographically they have much in common, linguistically they have many differences. The North Downs are their spinal column. The white chalk of these and of the white cliffs of Dover gave England its first recorded name of Albion. Between the North and South Downs lies the Weald, the Old English word for woodland, where the trees were felled by the tall fair-haired Saxons to produce a crop of place-names that not only date the clearings, but bear testimony to some of our earliest industries. It was the metal resources of the region that attracted the Romans, who lost little time in working the iron of the Weald as they were later to work the lead of the Mendips and Shropshire and the iron of the Forest of Dean.

Caesar's landing in the late August of 55 BC was both abortive and embarrassing. Ten thousand men sailed under a full moon from Boulogne; but a north-easterly gale wrecked many of the galleys and we have Caesar's own account of the difficulties encountered on landing near Deal.

Weighed down by heavy armour, his troops had to fight their way up the shelving beach that gave them no firm foothold on which to make a stand against the tribesmen, who appeared in unexpectedly large numbers, hurling their javelins as they galloped past on firm land with such effect that it quickly became apparent that the legionaries had no stomach for the undertaking. Caesar states frankly that they were terrified, although he also states that despite the disadvantages of the terrain it was really the failure of the cavalry transports to make shore in time that deprived him of a decisive victory. Whether this is true or false, the fact was that when he appreciated fully the ferocity of the tribesmen he was obliged to withdraw.

In the summer of the following year he returned with a larger force; but only to learn again how well-trained the tribesmen were. 'Their skill', he wrote, 'may be judged by the fact that they can control their horses at full gallop on the steepest incline, check and turn them in a moment, run along the pole, stand on the yoke, and get back into the chariot as quick as lightning'. The secret of their dexterity was that they got their living by hunting. They survived from an Iron-Age culture that, to our regret, left little decisive evidence in place-names; but from archaeological evidence we know that on the Sussex downs flints had been mined from an early date to provide primitive axe-heads for tree-felling, and that this had already enabled the tribesmen to get at the mineral wealth of the region. An old track across Riddlesdown in Surrey was used to reach the flint mines there in Neolithic times.

Caesar was not to be turned back a second time without achieving some sort of victory. So despite the cunning of the Belgic chieftain, Cassivelaunus, and the bravery of his followers, the legions pressed on through the Kentish Weald and up the marshes of the Thames Valley, to ford the river and advance northwards to Wheathampstead, where Cassivelaunus had his headquarters. Only there could the decisive blow be struck. At considerable cost the assault succeeded. The Belgic encampment was destroyed. But Cassivelaunus himself escaped and Caesar did not follow up the victory. He returned to Kent and again withdrew from the country, leaving Cassivelaunus to keep up the spirits of his warriors by fighting the Trinovantes. So of the 54 BC invasion the only impressive memorial remaining on land is the decayed ramparts of Caesar's base camp at Worth.

The full-scale invasion of Britain in 43 AD, and the place-name record, starts with places that no longer bear Roman names: Richborough, the great port of *Rutupiae*, a few miles from Sandwich, Reculver in the north, Dover in the south, and Lympne, a vanished seaport in Romney marsh. The flint walls at Richborough date from a period three centuries later than the Claudian invasion, reminding us that a fortress was raised there to defend the Romanised Britons from the men with winged helmets who sailed up the Thames in their long-ships from Denmark. The name, Dover, is derived from Dubris, the name of the stream that ran out into the sea there, which later became Dour, a name identical with the Welsh *dwfr*, 'water'. Even Reculver, the Roman *Regulbium*, comes from a British word meaning beak, or bill, and Canterbury itself, the Roman *Durovernum* is from Old English words meaning 'the bury of the people of Kent'. To the Saxons it was Cantwarabyrig.

Canterbury was chosen as a base because it stood at the lowest point at which the Stour could be forded, Rochester because it stood at the lowest point at which the Medway could be bridged. Both were vital to the strategy of the Roman invasion and key points in a road system that facilitated later invasions. So if place-name evidence is scanty, we have the roads to remind us of the vigour of that first century invasion. Three of these start respectively at Dover, Richborough, and Lympne, where Roman remains have been found, and all three converge on Canterbury. As roads and topographical features are better guides in general than place-names to the progress of an invader, we need not complain. It will be found over the country as a whole that invaders provide more conclusive evidence for determining place-names than place-names do for determining and dating invasions.

One wing of the invading army of 43 AD advanced westward under Vespasian to attack Mai Dun, a Belgic fortress, and eventually to storm Maiden Castle at Dorchester. Its progress was assisted by an agreement made with the king of the Verica which gave free passage for the legions through Sussex. This resulted in the Kingdom of Verica becoming a client-state under the Romans, and to its king being given the title of *Rex et Legatus Augusti*, as we are reminded by the inscription built into the wall of Chichester's Town Hall. Few readers will need reminding that Chichester, the county town of West Sussex, occupies the site of a Roman city, or that Bosham was a major port. The main body of the army, however, established itself in Canterbury and from there advanced upon London.

The unrelenting resurgence of Nature makes it impossible to assess the amount of woodland cleared by the Romans, but it was certainly considerable. The early place-names ending in -ing in the Roman villa country between Rochester and Maidstone suggest that the later invaders took advantage of clearings that already existed, and the early settlement of the open country in Thanet, particularly up the valleys towards Canterbury, makes it clear that the rivers as well as the roads provided early lines of communication here as they did in less heavily wooded counties. The place-name, Sturry, 'the Stour district', where a Saxon-Frisian cemetery was found, and Eastry, 'the eastern district', where the *villa regalis* of the Cantware stood, are both early, and there is evidence for early settlement in such place-names as Barming, Yalding, and Malling on the belt of fine arable soil near Maidstone to the south of the Downs. But for ordinary purposes it is true to say that away from the roads and rivers penetration into the Weald was slow. Most of the early settlement was in the north-east.

The degree to which the heavy forest of the Weald cut off Kent from the rest of southern England in early times is shown in the fact that so many of its place-names are as peculiar to the county as many in Cornwall are to the remote south-west, and the two names of Kent and Cornwall are closely akin. There is even place-name evidence that the Weald cut off the people of the north of Kent from those of the south. Lympne, Lyminge, and many others do not have obvious derivations and are peculiar to the one district. Despite the antiquity and early prosperity of such charming places as Billinghurst, Fernhurst and Midhurst, as late as 1902 there were still 125,000 acres of woodland in Sussex.

There is supporting evidence for this isolation in the survival of heathenism, even near Roman settlements. It continued so long that offerings to devils had to be specifically forbidden by King Wihtred in 685. There is evidence of the worship of Thunor among the Jutes of Kent, and of the cult of Woden in Woodnesborough, near Sandwich, and also in Wormshill between Maidstone and Faversham. Five places of heathen worship can even by identified by their names within a radius of twelve miles of Canterbury. Nor have Sussex and Surrey a better record in the story of conversion to Christianity. The Wey valley in Surrey has been described as a very pantheon of paganism, while Sussex, not unexpectedly, has a large proportion of heathen place-names. What makes this seem odd is that pre-Saxon place-names are extremely rare in both Kent and Sussex. The explanation is in the earliness of the alien settlement of these counties.

The division of Kent into Lathes gave the county an individuality that Bede tells us was Jutish, and brings it into relationship with Hampshire and the Isle of Wight. This is confirmed by the similarity between names in South Hampshire – such as Swaythling and Nursling – and many in Kent, and their difference from those of Sussex. But complications were introduced into the nomenclature of Kent by the Danes, who after earlier raids, such as the one at Bloody Point in Sandwich Bay, took up their winter quarters in Thanet for the first time in 857, and from there marched inland to plunder and burn Canterbury. Their place-names, however, are largely confined to the coast. In Ramsgate, Margate, Northgate, Sandgate, 'gate' is typically Scandinavian; but why, we may ask, does it become 'gut' in Romney Marsh? The answer is that the modification is dialectical. The guts are invariably ways to the sea, and suggest that streams, like men, are sometimes determined 'to gang their ain gate'; but many marshland names, such as Pluck's Gutter Bridge across the Stour, Farthinghoe, and Sugarloaf, near Ham Street, remain mysteries.

The chief interest of marshland names in Kent is in what they disclose about the fickle favours of the sea; but again we need to tread as warily among the names as we do on the marshes themselves. A ditch might be called a grave, so Graveney is 'island by a ditch', but Ebbesfleet may not mean 'ebbing fleet'. It may mean 'stream where the hips grow'. The Durlocks have an interest all their own. There is more than one in Kent, and the name is applied to the east cliffs at Folkestone. The word probably means somebody's enclosure, as we have it in Challock, 'enclosure for calves' in Kent, and Porlock, 'enclosure by the port', in Somerset. In the Isle of Oxney we have 'the Stocks'; near Appledore, 'the Dowels', which is a local word for marshes.

Winding courses had obviously to be taken across the marshes by herdsmen as well as by streams. So on the marshes of Thanet we have Snake Drove for a cattle trail, Sarre Penn for a water channel, the 'penn' indicating that the water was penned, or pent, between high banks. Sarre itself is an instance of the name of a stream being adopted by the town that developed on its bank, only to be sacked by the Danes in the ninth century. Behind Dymchurch Wall is Donkey Street. And so we might go on.

The best known reminders of the shifting soils and sands of the coast are Rye and Winchelsea. Rye means 'at an island', and formerly stood on an island in the estuaries of the Brede and the Tillingham. The middle part of Winchelsea is also from the Old English word for island. In its earliest form it meant 'island in or by the bend of the Brede'. The two towns have had different fates. Rye survived on its island knoll while the sea washed round it. The original Winchelsea was submerged and a new town laid on a chess-board plan that makes it unique in England, although it has a parallel in Wales.

Inland the chief characteristic of the place-names of Kent, now a county of hop gardens and oast-houses, is the great number of them that indicate how densely wooded the county was when the invaders came.

The -hursts, -leys, -fields, and -dens are permanent reminders of this density, which must have contributed to the survival of heathenism. South of the railway between Tonbridge and Ashford there is a concentration of -dens such as we find nowhere else – Benenden, Iden, Tenterden, Halden, Curtisden, Smarden, Horsmonden, Frittenden, Standen, Bethersden, Marden and many others. 'Den' means a woodland pasture for pigs, and Tenterden, 'the swine pasture of the people of Thanet', reminds us of the great herds that fed on the beech mast and acorns of these woodlands. The -leys are almost as numerous, but they are common throughout the whole of southern England, whereas the 'dens' with this meaning are almost confined to Kent and Sussex, although they are found elsewhere meaning dene. The charts are more significant: Chartwell, Chart Sutton, Chartham and the rest of them. They have the same meaning as Churt in Surrey. They denote a rough common overgrown with gorse, broom, or bracken, suggesting sterile soil.

Within an area of a few square miles in mid-Kent may be found more than a hundred names indicating an area of woodland – and, incidentally, they have their counterparts in such typically Kentish personal-names as Hayward, Woodward and Hogben. It has even been suggested by the irreverent that one origin of the noble name of Howard was hog-ward! Another local ending is -ett, which is usually prefixed with the name of a tree or plant. There are Rushetts in all these counties; Birchett in Kent means 'birch copse'. In all of them French influence is indicated.

In a countryside that was brought into cultivation late we should not expect many -ings; but what, we might ask, is the explanation of several place-names ending with -inge? Lyminge, Sellinge, and Hawkinge are examples. Ekwall tells us that -ge in Lyminge once denoted a large district, while Sellinge appears to be from the Old Frisian word for 'abode'. We find this archaic -ge ending also in Surrey, Ely and Essex. Another tricky name is Poulder, borne by the two farms, South and North Poulder. It is from a Dutch word meaning a reclaimed piece of ground, and this derivation may be thought to be confirmed when we find a place called Flemings, about a mile south of Ash. Norman-French names are rare in Kent. Wickhambreux is one of the few. But if we look across the Channel we see that the modern neighbourly twinning of towns is not as new as we may have thought. Earlier enthusiasts went much further than we do. They duplicated the names. So we have Sangatte –

Sandgate, Lozinhem – Lossingham, Wimille – Windmill, and Ham simply repeated.

As late as the fourteenth century, the Weald settlements were still mostly hamlets and isolated farmsteads; but gavelkind tenure, with multiple inheritance, which led to the breaking up of holdings on a death, appears to have produced more intensive cultivation of what land there was for crops.

Although the three counties of Kent, Sussex and Surrey hang together topographically they did not grow up, as it were, together. Kent and Sussex have, however, one great historic link that is of inexhaustible interest. The entire area of the Kent and Sussex 'hursts' bristles with reminders that this now fair and fertile land was once our English Black Country. And along with the iron works there were the glass works, usually situated on hill tops to catch the air currents needed to fan the furnaces. At least twenty-seven glass-making sites have been discovered in Sussex alone.

The 'Iron Age', in this sense of the term, finds real meaning in Sussex. For two thousand years it flourished, reaching its peak in Tudor and Stuart times. The blast furnaces required a good head of water to work the bellows, and some idea of the Sussex scene is to be found in Camden's *Britannia* (1586) where he writes: 'there be furnaces on every side . . . to which purpose divers brooks in many places are brought to run in one channel, and sundry meadows turned into pools and waters, that they might be of power sufficient to drive hammer mills, which beating upon the iron, resound all over the places adjoining.' These hammer ponds, strung along the rivers, are an impressive sight from the air. There are eleven on streams running down to Heathfield Furnace, one of the most prosperous. Many of these beautiful expanses of water, now so placid, can be seen from the high ground of St. Leonards Forest, from which timber was taken to feed the furnaces. Newbridge, Newpound in Wisborough Green, and Cross-in-Hand on Waldron Down, were hamlets of iron-workers. The iron masters built some of the finest houses in Sussex, including Batemans in Burwash, the home of Rudyard Kipling.

The typical ending in the iron-smelting region, -hurst, seems to mean something more precise than wood – perhaps the wood from which timber was taken. Certainly Staplehurst must mean wood from which staples, or posts, were cut, and the 'hursts' of Kent and Sussex were the woods from which timber was taken to feed the furnaces, of which there are innumerable reminders in both counties. Cranbrook, the capital of the Kentish Weald, was an iron-smelting centre before it became famous for its orchards. In the Goudhurst-Hawkhurst region we find such names as Furnace Farm and Three Chimneys Farm, on which iron must have been worked since the beginning of recorded time. The most prosperous of all the Kentish iron works were at Lamberhurst. Colliers Green and Collier Street were where the charcoal burners had their hearths.

When we cross into Sussex we find reminders of iron works at Old Forge in Maresfield, Forge Farm and Wood in Wadhurst, and Forge Wood in Burwash. Furnace Wood at Heathfield still has the remains of an old iron mill and a sluice-gate and culvert from the original hammer pond. And the word 'hammer' occurs in Hammerden, which appears to be from the forge hammer. If so, Judith Glover, in her valuable work on Sussex place-names, says that it must have been the first recorded in Sussex, since all the -dens were ancient enclosures. Hammerwoods at Forest Row, Lindfield, and Ardingly refer to early iron works, while in Ashburnham, on the bank of the river Ashbourne, we have a reminder of the need of water to power the great drop-hammers used in the iron industry. Most of these workings are ancient. We know, for example, that at Huggett's Furnace at Buxted on the edge of Ashdown Forest – stripped of timber to feed the furnaces – iron was worked at least as early as Vespasian.

For clues to early lines of settlement along inland routes we follow the downland trackways that captivated the imaginations of Kipling and Belloc, and Belloc's Halnaker, incidentally, is an abridgement of half-an-acre, which local humour is said to have rendered 'half-naked' for three hundred and fifty years. Most of the Iron Age forts on the Downs lacked the basic necessities of life, but villages would later be developed wherever the water gushed from the chalk, as it does in so many places. The land near the village could be cultivated to a limited degree; but the main source of livelihood on the Downs was the flocks of sheep turned out to graze on their turf and water at the dewponds that are so characteristic a feature of the Sussex scene. In course of time drovers' roads, following the easiest lines through the Weald, would be trodden out by the herds and flocks being driven through the woods to the fertile land on the coastal plain, where the cattle would be fattened for sale in the market towns that were eventually to become the pleasant small towns so much favoured by the well to do in the south of the county. In the neighbourhood of Billinghurst these drove roads seem surprisingly straight until we realise that they are running parallel to the Roman Stane Street. Some of these tracks took advantage of gaps in the Downs, or terraces along their slopes, as at Steyning and Storrington. Many survive as green lanes, the breadth of which provides evidence of the size of the flocks that were formerly driven along them. The Findon Gap was so favoured a route by the drovers that Horsham market developed to avoid the necessity of so long a journey.

As the woodland was steadily cut back, or reduced by the saplings being torn down by the oxen -always greedy feeders – swine pastures similar to those of Kent were established, particularly in the West Sussex neighbourhood of Worthing, where we find them at Durrington, Ferring, West Tarring and Washington, all incorporating the early -ing ending. The way the drovers avoided the marshes is seen in the old track that links Amberley with Rackham, curving away from the Arun to survive as a greenway to Wisborough Green. These -dens, or swine pastures, were usually located near streams, because they were used by men as well as beasts. They were the bases from which the Saxons went out to clear the timber further inland.

The early settlements in east Sussex are closely related to those of Kent. The Haestingas took their name from their leader, *Haesta*, and gave their folk name to Hastings, their capital settlement. The reason for their remaining so closely-knit a community was that they occupied an area of dry land cut off by Romney Marsh to the east and Pevensey Marsh to the west, while inland lay the forest, which they were the first of the Saxon invaders to attack with determination, again showing how much greater the difficulty of draining the marshes was than that of felling the trees. This resulted in the many elongated parishes on the coastal side of the South Downs which run up into the downland itself. These must have given the Haestingas a range of land that supported their characteristic self-sufficiency, and made them in that respect comparable with the Scandinavian settlers in the North of England so much later. They had arable land near their main settlement, with grazing for oxen and pigs inland, and beyond that they had sheep walks on the Downs. Just as Thanet had its swine pastures at Tenterden, Washington was an important manor with pastures distributed across a broad area of the Weald, ranging in distance up to twenty miles from the ancient '-ton of Wassa's people'. But these pastures were not called 'dens' in Sussex, except along the Kent border. They were called -folds, a name which indicates that they were staked off. We find them in such names as Slinfold, 'fold on the slope of a hill', Cowfold, which is self-explanatory, and Chiddingfold in Surrey, 'the fold of Cida's people'.

Sussex, as a county favoured by people of culture and leisure, is well endowed with studies of its history and antiquities. Such a summary of its most characteristic features as this must seem sketchy to those who have studied the place-names of the South-East in detail.

The topographical approach certainly becomes inadequate when we try to understand the character of the many small hamlets in west Sussex, few of which are centred in large villages or small market towns. It would require an expert on early charters to account for them. All we can say here is that their explanation appears to lie in the size of the great Saxon multiple-estates of West Sussex, which appear to have had histories going back to pre-Roman times, and even in some cases to have been connected with hill forts on the hills above them. It has been pointed out that the largest of these multiple-estates had its headquarters at Findon, immediately below Cissbury, the finest of the Sussex hill-forts, which takes its name from the Cissa who gave his name to Chichester. So while we can explain most place-name patterns in relation to successive invaders, in this part of Sussex the origins are much more complex.

The settlement of Sussex from the sea started with an invasion in the last quarter of the fifth century that was entirely independent of the invasions that resulted in the creation of the kingdoms of Kent to the east and Wessex to the west. This separateness of Sussex, which has boundaries more clearly defined than those of any other county, is seen at once in land divisions as we pass from the Lathes of Kent to the Rapes of Sussex. At the same time there are equally curious similarities in some of the place-names of the two counties that have no counterparts elsewhere. One of these is in the first syllable of Hoathley, which means a heather-covered clearing, or heath. Shoreham in Sussex – really Old Shoreham – 'the ham at a rock or steep slope', from the Old English *scora*, the source of the word 'shore', is found again at Shorne in Kent. By distinction, the element 'glind' found in four Sussex place-names, is found nowhere else in England. It is from Middle Low German and means fenced enclosure.

In Sussex and Essex there is a complete dearth of pre-Saxon place-names. This used to be attributed to the extermination by the Saxons of the Romano-British population already there, an explanation that is no longer tenable. It seems much more reasonable to assume that the true explanation is the completeness of the Saxon occupation of territory that had previously been poor and sparsely populated. Sussex, even more than Essex, is the county in which the -ingas ending can usefully be studied. Around Pevensey, and extending eastward as far as Chichester Harbour, the kingdom of the South Saxons was established. To the north and west of this territory we find place-names ending in -ey, Chilley, Fortheye, Horse-eye and Rickney, showing that the marshes of the Pevensey Levels in Roman times must have been a saltmarsh over which the tide flowed to produce an archipelago of small islands. This would account for a break in the line of early settlements, although the antiquity of the great drainage channel, Mark Dyke, is proved by its being the boundary along its entire length between the Pevensey and Hastings Rapes.

Apart from this break, the earliness of the South Saxon settlement along the entire coastal strip is shown in the density of the -ing endings. It is the densest to be found anywhere in England, although few are found on the downland round Eastbourne, Lewes and Brighton. There are more than three times as many of them in Sussex as in Kent. Lancing, Steyning, Sompting, Goring, Angmering, Wittering, Worthing are only a few of the well-known examples, and cemeteries connected with many of these early settlements are found all along the chalk downs inland – as they are also found on the Downs where few -ing endings occur. The cemetery at High Down, Ferring, and pottery found at Alfriston show that the coastal areas of Sussex were occupied by the Saxons before 500. Other burial places have been identified at Eastbourne, Hassocks, Patcham, and Saddlescombe. In all, forty-five places ending originally in the plural *-ingas* are to be found either near the coast or accessible from a river. The next group in order of antiquity, the *-inghams*, lies away from the coast but near streams. When we reach the Weald we find such pagan names as Whyly in East Hoathley and Wiligh in Ticehurst, which confirms the belief that the heathen Germanic tribes placed their sanctuaries in the depth of forests.

The name Woolbeding, near Midhurst, shows how far inland the Saxons were able to sail up the waterways, although perhaps the most remarkable fact about Sussex river-names is that one of the most important, the Adur, did not receive its present name until 1622, when Michael Drayton published his *Polyolbion*, a topographical description of England, and mistook the mouth of the river at Shoreham for the Roman harbour of *Portus Adurni*, which correctly gave its name to Portsmouth.

Another important Sussex river, the Arun, did not acquire its present name until the thirteenth century. Its old name was Tarente, meaning trespasser and referring to its habit of flooding its valley. The name Arundel, 'horehound valley', is from a plant of the deadnettle family which must have grown here profusely, but seems an odd name to give to either the river or the town that sprang up round the noblest of all the baronial strongholds of Sussex, which like Lewes commanded a gap through the Downs and, again like Lewes, gave rise to a town that was once a thriving port for timber.

The tendency of the Sussex rivers to flood may account for some of the general lack of early names near them. We may think of the frequency with which the minor name 'strood', meaning marshy ground or ground overgrown with brushwood, appears on large-scale maps. We meet it at farms in Wivelsfield, Ardingly, Chiddingly, Cuckfield, Petworth, and Wisborough Green, where Wisborough itself means 'marsh by marshy meadow'. Storrington is 'storks farmstead', and is another instance of the town giving its name to the river, not of the more usual opposite. The pools at Parham were formerly famous for the heron colonies.

There are many examples in Sussex of place-names which suggest that the South Saxons were unlike other Saxons in their naming of places. We have instances in Brede and Shulbrede, in which 'brede' means breadth in the sense of a plain or wide expanse. Shulbrede meant 'strip of land on a slope'. The word *leon* from which Heene in Worthing is derived is from a lost cognate of the Old English *hiwan* meaning 'household or family'. All these examples are supporting evidence of the early date at which Sussex south of the Downs was settled by the Saxons.

The most notable feature administratively is the division of the county into six Rapes. This again is unique. It derives from the Old English *rap*, 'rope'. Why? we may ask. It could never have been possible to put a rope round the whole of a Rape. Does it mean that 'rope' was used in the sense of a line? It seems more probable that the word was introduced because the place in which the original open-air courts were held would be roped off. These enclosures may have come to be called rapes, and eventually the name to be applied to the area not of the actual court but of its jurisdiction. As we shall see, this grouping of settlements round an administrative centre had its parallels in the shires, which took their name from the town from which they were administered.

Surrey, when compared with Sussex and Kent, may appear to lack unity. The chalk ridge that runs through Guildford and along the Hog's

Back divides the county by separating the towns to the north from those to the south; and those to the south are further split in that the affinities at the eastern end are with Kent, at the western end with Hampshire, and in the middle with Sussex. Geographically, we might feel that the same basic considerations apply to Surrey as to Kent in that the pre-historic highway, the Harroway, which means 'hard road', started in Kent and continued along the southern escarpment of the North Downs until eventually it reached Stonehenge and Salisbury Plain. Today part of it is called The Pilgrims' Way, and we are sometimes told that it was established for the use of pilgrims to Canterbury; but long before Canterbury became a place of pilgrimage this ancient trackway was used by pilgrims travelling in the opposite direction to Stonehenge.

Communication between north and south was provided for by water gaps made by the Darent, the Wey and the Mole, of which roads and railways have now taken advantage, and when a direct route was required along a route not lined out by a waterway, dips in the chalk ridge, sometimes called wind-gaps, were used. Reigate, situated below a steep escarpment, is the outstanding example of a town that achieved importance by reason of being at the crossing of the Harroway and the trackway through the Merstham Gap.

In general, the lines of early settlement in Surrey follow the normal course in that they are along the rivers. So we find Woking and Godalming on the Wey, Dorking on the Mole, Tooting on the Wandle; and in the south-west corner, when we penetrate into what was formerly forest, we reach a pocket of pre-Christian names, such as Peper Harow, Thursley, and Willwy in Farnham, while at Drakeshill, south of Guildford, there is a mound capped by the chapel of St. Catherine, an example of a heathen site being consecrated to Christian worship. Tuesley in Godalming contains the Tiw element found in the third day of the week, and there is a Thunderfield in Horley. All these bear testimony to the kind of settlements that long continued in the heathland between Surrey and the old settlements of Wessex. Farnham means 'ham where the ferns grow', which does not suggest an area of high fertility.

Nowhere in Surrey is there place-name evidence of Jutish influences such as are found in Hampshire. The towns in the west are late and began as offshoots. Haslemere, for example, was first mentioned as late as 1180, when it appeared as an offshoot of Chiddingfold, itself an offshoot of Godalming. Scandinavian and Norman influences are minimal. The county has no Norman castles. But, incidentally, the word 'offshoot' is a reminder that there is one interesting link between the place-names of Surrey and those of Hampshire. It is in the 'shotts', a place-name element not common elsewhere. A shott is a projecting piece of land – a shoot – and is common on the Berkshire border. Oxshott is an example in Surrey. The curious feature about the 'shot' ending is the frequency with which it is found prefixed by the name of a tree, as in Aldershot, Bramshott (bramble), Ewshott (yew), Spurshott (pear). In Empshott, as an exception, the 'emp' stands for a swarm of bees.

Perhaps we are wrong in looking for unity in Surrey's relationships with counties to the south and west. The name of the county means 'southern district', so we might ask how it stands in relation to the counties north of the Thames. The answer, unfortunately, is that there are few Surrey names that we can relate to names in Buckinghamshire or Middlesex, and when we take into account that the river must have been an effective barrier, and that both the north and south banks of the upper reaches of the Thames retained large tracts of forest until comparatively recent times, the connection between Surrey and its neighbours to the north in pre-Norman days does not look at all convincing. It may to some extent be argued that Surrey was the counterpart in the south to the Chilterns in the north; but that contributes little to explaining why it was called the southern district, because it fails to answer the question: 'southern to what?' It may be that we are asking a question to which there is no answer because it is not a valid question. Perhaps Surrey never was thought of as a social unit. It certainly never had any racial unity. The only even allegedly Celtic name in the county is Penge, although Beddington as a name might suggest that a lost tribe called the Beddings formerly roamed these parts. Walton-on-Thames, Walworth and Wallington have British first elements; but these are minor points that do not explain why so large an area should have come to be the southern district. It may well be that the name should have been 'the southern way' or something of that kind, since the one feature that holds the region together is the Harroway.

Seen purely in relation to the Thames, many of the places in north Surrey have great historical significance. Most of the waterside villages have names that go back to Saxon times, and we recall that Kingston-upon-Thames was the place where seven Saxon kings were crowned, and that Chertsey, 'Cerot's island', had an abbey founded by Erconwald in the third quarter of the seventh century and richly endowed by the Mercian kings. And what shall we say of Shepperton? No-one would think of it as the shepherds' town to-day, which is what the name signifies; but Shepperton better than most Thames-side villages preserves the memory of its past. Tumuli at War Close are believed by many to be connected with the Roman crossing of the Thames in 54 BC which was where our account of these three counties began. So perhaps there is some sort of unity after all. We found it between Kent and Sussex in the hammer ponds and woodland clearings. Surrey, too, has its hammers, of which the best known is Abinger Hammer, and in thinking of the three counties as a region we may be thankful that whatever the twentieth century has done to spoil much of England, in the south-east we are able to take comfort in the reflection that an industry as little associated with beauty as iron-smelting has left us, not slag heaps, but lovely hammer ponds and the fine half-timbered houses of the old iron-masters.

CHAPTER TWO

Southern England

HAMPSHIRE · BERKSHIRE · WILTSHIRE DORSET

Hampshire is a regal and ecclesiastical county. Winchester, once the national capital, has a proud place in history that gives this oldest of the Shires a dignity all its own. Immediately before the Norman Conquest Edward the Confessor was its chief landowner. He held estates at Basingstoke, Andover, Wymering, Porchester, Rockbourne, King's Somborne, Titchfield and Twyford. His queen drew revenues from other estates, and her father, the Earl of Wessex, as well as her brothers, were Hampshire landowners. Since the Conquest the dominant influence has been the bishopric of Winchester, of which Thomas Fuller wrote: 'Canterbury's the higher rack, but Winchester's the better manger'.

The mediaeval diocese was vast. It included the county of Surrey, hence the palace at Farnham. There were other palaces at Taunton in Somerset and at Bishop's Waltham. At Highclere, in the north of the county, the bishop had a great manor house from which a large estate was administered, bringing wealth from the wool produced by the flocks of sheep put out to graze in the valley between Beacon Hill and Sidown Hill, and sold to the rich clothiers of Newbury. Bishop's Sutton and Bishopstoke are two other place-names reminding us of this widely cast ecclesiastical influence. Burghclere was another place belonging to the bishop. He had a market there.

The third 'clere', Kingsclere, was obviously a royal manor. Its pride is that it was one of the possessions of King Alfred, who marshalled Wessex against the Viking invaders. These three 'cleres' lie south of the river Enborne, and it seems probable that their name means 'bright stream' and suggests that this was the former name of the river. If this is so, it indicates that we have another instance of a stream giving its name to a district. Place-names derived from a stream are found again in the -inge group, Wantage (King Alfred's birth place), Lockinge, and Ginge between the Berkshire Downs and the Upper Thames. They suggest that men of an ancient race reached this part of Berkshire, and also of Hampshire, by advancing up the Thames in the sixth century following their earlier settlement in north Kent. Reverting for a moment to ecclesiastical influences in the region, it is worth mentioning that the influence of the bishops of Winchester in this part of Hampshire had its counterpart in neighbouring Berkshire, where eight place-names between Sonning and the Hampshire border, all British, do not appear in Domesday. They are Wokingham, Ruscombe, Winnersh, Woodcray, Woodley, Sandford, Sandhurst and Sindlesham. The reason for their omission is that they were part of the Bishop of Salisbury's manor of Sonning, to which their revenues were payable. When commenting on the smallness of the hamlets with no obvious centre in a large village or town in coastal Sussex, it was suggested that this was due to remote administration by a large landowner. It may be at least feasible that the many small hamlets in Hampshire were affected in the same way by being administered from Winchester.

These understandable links between Hampshire and its neighbours do not, however, affect the deep-seated differences between Wessex and the Kingdom of the South Saxons. A cursory glance at the map might suggest that British survival was strong in Hampshire. If we look again we see that most of the towns and villages with British names take them from the rivers on which they stand. A fisherman would say that this needs no explaining when we look at the Avon, the Itchen and the Test; but the associations predate this favoured position. Andover, in which the first syllable refers to Anton, a tributary of the Test, Candover, and Micheldever are all from British river names adopted by Saxon settlers. Mich- in Micheldever, where a pagan cemetery was found, has the same root as 'Much' in the names of towns and villages found elsewhere in the South. The second part of all these names is from the British *dubris*, 'water', as we have it in Dover. Another Hampshire name, Wallop, found in Nether and Over Wallop, is from *waell-hop*, 'valley of the stream'.

For an explanation of this characteristic of the county we only need to bear in mind the fine natural harbours from which so many navigable rivers fan out across the map. The Meon was the river up which the Jutes sailed, and names like Thunor's Grove, with counterparts in Kent, indicate that there was a cult for his worship among the Jutes, which found its last expression topographically in Hampshire. The town from which the county takes its name occupies a peninsula formed by the Itchen and the Test, and here we find that the Roman settlement was at Bitterne, a name derived from the two words *aern* 'house' and *byht* 'bend', which is a reference to the horse-shoe shaped ridge nearby. The development of Southampton received a set-back during the Viking raids, but it got its charter from King Ethelwulf in 840. Portsmouth does not appear as a port at Domesday. It only developed as such when the approaches to Roman Porchester began to silt up.

From Southampton the raiders advanced to Winchester, already important as a tribal capital of the Belgae, with a pagan cemetery on St. Giles's Hill. To the Romans it was *Venta Belgarum*, to the Saxons Wintanceaster. The Romans constructed a road from Porchester to Winchester, the southern section of which has disappeared except for fragments, and from Winchester itself five roads were constructed (in addition to the one linking it with Porchester). One went north-east to Silchester, the only town in Britain that has an indisputably Roman church, another left the city on the north to join the road from London to Bath, one went due south to the port of Clausentum, near Bitterne, the fourth due west to Old Sarum.

Despite these communications there are few obviously early place-names in the centre and north of Hampshire. Clearly there was no widespread advance by Saxon invaders across the county during the first half of the sixth century. The only -ing endings between Winchester and the Berkshire border are Basing and Worting, both folk names. Basing was one of Harold's manors, and owes much of its early importance to its situation in a gap in the chalk, which provided passage between the Thames and the Hampshire basins. This strategic importance was recognised by the Normans when they built a castle there. Odiham, another place with a castle, was 'wooden ham' and raises the question of how the 'w' came to be dropped. It was probably due to the Norman difficulty with that letter. The original settlement, of course, was round the keep on the river bank.

When we examine the -tons we find that several were near the sources of rivers up which the invaders had advanced by degrees. Alton stands near the head waters of the Wey. It is 'the ton at the source of the river', just as Alton Pancras in Dorset is 'the -ton at the source of the Piddle' and Alton Barnes and Alton Priors -tons at the source of the Avon. The original Alton acquired prosperity later as a halting place on the pilgrim route from Winchester to Canterbury. Near it is the village of Holybourne, another reminder of the pilgrims mentioned in *Piers Plowman*:

> Ye, thorough the pass of Aultone
> Poverte myght pass
> Withouten peril of robbynge.

To the south is Oakhanger, 'oak wood on a slope'. An escarpment runs north-south across the county, and here we are in Gilbert White country. A footpath leads up from Selborne to the Common, now National Trust property. And at Clanfield, 'clean field', lived the family of Edward Gibbon, who wrote of it: 'The downs commanded a noble prospect, and the long hanging woods in sight of the house could not perhaps have been improved by art or expense'. Clandon, a name found also in Surrey, means land cleared of the bushes and shrubs normally found on heathland.

Perhaps the most important of these trackway towns in Hampshire is Andover, which sprang up at the crossing of two Roman roads, the Portway from Silchester to Old Sarum and the one running from Winchester to Cirencester. From this crossing developed a market town in Saxon times, and later the great centre for wool from the sheep sold at Weyhill Fair. And it is worth mentioning that despite the importance of swine pastures in this heavily wooded county, the Hampshire hog is not a pig, but a hoggett, a sheep.

In the south of the county we have in Christchurch another historic town built between streams. From the place-name point of view, Christchurch lost its topographical identity when it abandoned its earlier name of Twynham, which meant 'the place between streams' and duplicated Twineham in Sussex. Its present name came only with the foundation of the great priory in the eleventh century by Edward the Confessor. The other New Forest priory, that at Romsey, 'Rum's island', was a Benedictine nunnery dating from the tenth century. Another significant New Forest name is Ringwood, probably from *rima*, 'border', indicating the Forest boundary, and two others that are, perhaps, of even greater significance are the Baddesleys found on either side of the Winchester to Romsey road, rare if not sole reminders that this may have been the name of the region before it became the New Forest under the Normans.

Crossing the Downs from Andover we enter Berkshire, with Newbury and all the shrunken towns and villages round it reminding us of the once prosperous clothing industry and 'Jack of Newbury'. To the east is Reading, the county town, where one of the earliest and most powerful

Benefictine abbeys flourished. Again we are in Thames-side country, with a string of fascinating small towns on both banks of the river. Upstream is Wallingford, occupying a strategic position where the London to Gloucester road forded the river before the mediaeval bridge with the fourteen arches was built. As 'the ford of Wealh's people' it was important in both Saxon and Norman England. The huge earthen rampart and ditch thrown up by the Saxons still encloses the town on three sides. They were constructed as defences against an enemy approaching along the Icknield Way from the Chilterns to attack Wessex.

Windsor as a name is identical with Winsor in Hampshire and the second parts of Broadwindsor and Little Windsor in Dorset. It obviously indicates a landing place, since *ora* meant bank or shore. It sprang up in a fertile stretch of country that early attracted settlement, and the fact that so many towns hereabouts remained attractively small was due to the size of the estates. The great manor of Sonning has been mentioned. Reading at Domesday covered an area at least seven miles wide, while on the Oxfordshire bank of the Thames the great manor of Bensingas, later known as Bensington or Benson, covered the whole of the fertile country between Henley and Dorchester.

Topographically there is little to distinguish Berkshire from Hampshire. Both have charming small towns, chalk downs and rich pastoral valleys. The Downs that dominate the country scene stimulate the imagination to visualise the countryside when the valleys would be swamps during much of the year, but when the sheep grazing on the Downs would still bring great wealth to their owners, often clerical. They would be driven in great flocks to such fairs as the famous August Fair at East Ilsley. Lambourn, now associated with racehorses, takes its name from the stream in which the lambs were washed, and it is by no means an irresponsible speculation to suggest that the names beginning with 'Bag' – such as Bagley, Bagnor and Bagshot in Surrey originated in a lost name for a wether or ram, since in Scandinavian languages *bagge* means 'ram'. It is worth noting that in the southern counties 'Bag' is always followed by a syllable descriptive of a natural feature, a ley, a shot, a wood, and never by a -ham, -ton, or -wic to suggest an inhabited place.

There are scholars who maintain that in Berkshire, Hampshire, Dorset and Somerset survivors are still to be seen of an ancient race completely different from the Celts surviving to the west. They are the tall, taciturn, slow-moving men with clear-cut features and aquiline noses found working the land here. Thomas Hardy saw their noble features as evidence of aristocratic forbears. They are more likely to be counterparts of the Cumbrian 'statesmen' Wordsworth admired so much, and to have originated in the free ceorls found living in Wessex and Mercia with no overlord to control them as early as the seventh century. They are mentioned in a passage in the Laws of Ine, giving them rights and duties in relation to enclosures.

This passage provides a clue to the agrarian system that continued into mediaeval times, and may explain the many names that contain 'carl' or charl', such as Carlton and Charlton. On the other hand, it could be that such names as these meant simply that not all workers in these districts were so privileged. We do, however, know that when the Saxons occupied Wessex there were many free peasants of British descent possessing as much as five hides of land although one hide was the usual holding of the ceorl, five hides of a thegn. The name Fyfield, found in all these counties, preserves the memory of the five-hide units measured out in these valleys for cultivation by ox-teams.

Wiltshire has its fertile valleys and villages that are fitting neighbours to those of Hampshire and Berkshire. Of seventy-five 'worths' in Wiltshire fifty-four are personal. But these are not the first images that spring to mind when Wiltshire is mentioned. Rather do we think of ancient trackways like the Icknield Way that runs by Whitehorse Hill and Wayland's Smithy towards Avebury, and the many prehistoric sites along its course. Silbury Hill, near Avebury, is surely one of the noblest of our ancient monuments. The massive monoliths found in Wiltshire, the dolmens, long barrows and – most important of all, the stone circles of Avebury and Stonehenge – are evidence of the strength of the megalithic culture of these ridgeway counties. It is a strange thought that the Salisbury Plain area, now among the most sparsely populated to be found anywhere in England, was the home of powerful tribes two thousand years before the Romans came. The windblown desolation of these heights in winter makes the evidence of the wealth of those who occupied them so long all the more impressive.

Even in Roman times the most populous parts of the region were the chalk uplands of Salisbury Plain, Berkshire, Dorset, and to a lesser degree of Hampshire. The river valleys that cut through the plateau were still uninhabited. Our present-day main roads are reminders of these times to tens of thousands of motorists making their way across the Plain to the West country resorts; but for those who have an eye for such things, the most fascinating part of these journeys is in the remnants to be seen on every hand of green roads and bridleways many of which are picked up for part of their length by lanes that link the highways with the villages of the Plain. The name 'Ox Drove' preserves the memory of one of them. Another green road runs for fifteen miles across the Plain, passing Winklebury Camp and Clearbury Ring. Some of the Iron Age camps in these parts were used for sheep and cattle fairs until these were superseded in modern times by cattle marts. A pierced sarsen stone used by ninth-century surveyors is mentioned in the charter by which King Egbert granted land at Alton Priors to the church of S.S. Peter and Paul at Winchester. We know that Ashmore, on a hill top south-east of Shaftesbury in Dorset, is the lineal descendant of a British settlement. The name of the village is Saxon, 'the pond by the ash tree', and the pond is still there; but the village was already old when the Saxons came. There are no characteristics of the place-names of Wiltshire which suggest that the expansion of the West Saxons into the region began before the middle of the sixth century, when the West Saxon king defeated the Britons of Old Sarum.

The Anglo-Saxon Chronicle has an account of two great fights between Wessex and Mercia. Tradition maintained that one of these was at Wanborough in Wiltshire. Now it is held that this battle was fought at Alton Priors (Wodensbeorg) and that a barrow called Adam's Grave marks the site.

Moving out of Wiltshire into Dorset, which took its name from the Durotriges, we find little in the district south of Shaftesbury to distinguish the one county from the other. It is only when we cross an imaginary line between Beaminster and Blandford that we sense the quintessential Dorset, and what character it has! It has its hill camps like those of Wiltshire, and boasts the greatest of all the tribal centres of these counties in Maiden Castle, Dorchester, the most massive prehistoric fortress in England, with a history going back at least to 2000 BC. But as our one interest in this book is the place-names thrown up by these ancient races as they infiltrated into the country, we always proceed with one eye on the map, and what fun these Dorset place-names are! Perhaps the prize should go to Toller Porcorum, in which the meaning of the surname, as it were, is obvious enough, and it is a characteristic of Dorset place-names that they do have what might be called surnames. Many of these are impressive. Whereas in some parts of the country saint's names tend to distinguish one village in a group from another, in Dorset they tend to be distinguished by the proud names of Norman landowners. Even Winterborne St. Andrew's became Winterborne Anderson. There are, however, the Minsters: Beaminster, Charminster, Iwerne Minster, Sturminster Marshall, Sturminster Newton, Yetminster, and Wimborne Minster, from which semi-collegiate groups of priests ministered over extensive territories, and there were many such churches that did not acquire minster naming – Sherborne, for example.

We do not know when the West Saxons first settled in Dorset. The use of British river names for early Saxon settlements suggests that it was not earlier than the seventh century. The villages along the tributaries of the Stour, for example, add the names of their owners to British river names. The Tarrants – there are eight of them – derive their names from a stream which bears a name closely related to the earlier name of the Arun and the Trent. Seven of them bear an owner's name. The exception is Tarrant Crawford, 'crow's ford'. Among the Piddles, or Puddles, is that curious name Piddletrenthide, which means 'Piddle of the thirty hides', trente being French for thirty. The Tollers – Toller Fratrum and Toller Porcorum – are so called because Toller was an early descriptive name for the river Tooke. If we question this we have to explain how the name Toller Whelme came to exist near the source of the Hooke, since this means 'the source of the Toller'. The name is found also in Tollard Farnham and Tollard Royal. The *toll* part is British and means 'pierced with holes', the *ardd* 'hill'. Toller Fratrum got its name from its ownership by Forde Abbey, which is yet another instance of Norman ownership being recorded, as we find it again in Stour Provost and Stour Paine, the one being a perversion of Prewes, from Preaux in Normandy, the other of Pagan, son of William the Conqueror.

This feature of Dorset names – the combination of British and Norman elements – which will be found also in Somerset and Devon, shows how much of the fertile land of the south-west was taken over by the Norman barons. The Nevill family is represented in the name of Fifehead Nevill (fife head being five hides) and the Peverells in at least four place names, while the Fitzpains make four appearances and the Matravers (Maltravers) five.

The Winterbornes are found in both Wiltshire and Dorset. The significance of the name is that it so picturesquely tells us that the chalk streams on the Wiltshire and Dorset Downs ran in winter, when the ground was saturated with autumn rains and the water level rose, to fall back again in summer. They are found in two groups in Dorset, one near the Frome watershed, the other near Blandford. Nearly all bear the names of Norman lords. The Wiltshire Winterbornes tend to be more 'churchy'. Winterborne Abbas belonged to the abbey of Cerne, Winterborne Came to the abbey of Caen in Normandy, Winterborne Monkton to the monks of the abbey of St. Vaast in Arras, while Winterborne Steepleton takes its name more modestly from the church steeple, and Winterborne Strickland, not from the Stricklands of Westmorland, but from *sticelan lane*, 'the steep path'.

The grouping of villages may be taken as characteristic of Norman overlordship. No doubt they were organised in this way for convenience of control. Hutchins, the Dorset historian, says: 'There are in Domesday Book nine manors or parcels of land surveyed by the name of Caundel, but there are no marks of distinction to ascertain any of them except Purse Caundel.' The Caundle referred to is now a brook with many streamlets running into it; but it is, as Leland reported, enclosed by well wooded hilly ground. The Norman element in place-names seldom appears before the thirteenth century.

Despite the lateness of the occupation, eighty *per cent* of Dorset's place-names are Saxon. Christopher Taylor, in the Dorset volume of 'The Making of the English Landscape' series says, 'for perhaps over two hundred and fifty years after the end of Roman rule most of Dorset remained a Romano-British rather than a Saxon sphere of influence, and in some parts rather longer.' The British language was not quite extinct in Dorset in the ninth century, yet only one *per cent* of the place-names in the county are entirely British. The reason, or reasons, for the slowness of the Saxon conquest may be found to be complicated by factors that did not worry the Romans unduly. This has to be said, because the question must inevitably be asked: 'Why did the Saxons not make use of the system of communications provided by the Romans?' Over twelve sites of Roman occupation have been discovered in the Yeo Valley near Sherborne; nearly fifty in the Isle of Purbeck.

Probably the main reason for Saxon delay was utilitarian. They were looking for good land to settle on. The inhospitable character of so much of the Dorset coast would be a restraining factor. There was access from Poole Bay, but the land they would see even there would not be thought attractive. So only the bolder spirits would press on up the river Stour until they reached the fertile valleys of the north-east.

The main landings of Saxons on the south coast in the fifth and sixth centuries had been in the Southampton-Portsmouth area. From there, as we have seen, they had been able to make their way up the rivers so successfully that eventually they had been able to link up with Saxons who had come into the region from the Thames valley. So by the end of the sixth century all Wessex to the east of Dorset was occupied, and the question was which line of advance offered the greatest advantages. The answer appeared to be Somerset, particularly as Gloucestershire to the north was already occupied. The vast extent of the heathlands of east Dorset and of the New Forest, as it is now called, beyond them must have been a major deterrent.

Looking towards the north we must ask what there was to impede entry from Wiltshire. The answer to this question is the Bokerley Dyke, which extends from Cranborne Chase along the county boundary for a distance of six miles until it reaches the heathlands of Dorset. This dyke was constructed about 370 AD to block the Dorchester-Salisbury Roman road at the time of the earlier Saxon raids. So it is not as surprising as it might have appeared that the Romano-British population remained undisturbed. There was only Poole Bay to provide access on a massive scale, and there we have Wareham, 'the ham by the weir'. What the early history of the settlement may have been I do not know. The massive earthworks known as 'the Walls' are said to have been erected by the Saxons in the ninth century to defend the town against the Vikings. But having regard to the vulnerability of Dorchester if this entry remained undefended, one would expect to find that its defences are much earlier than the ninth century. It is not, however, for me to venture into the field of scholars on such a question. I can only suggest that every place-name question in this region must be examined in relation to Dorchester, the county town, which not only occupies the site of the Roman town, but also of the great tribal capital of the Durotriges, Maiden Castle.

The impression made by Maiden Castle on a first visit is one that can never be forgotten, and provides a clue to the haunting sense of the past and the unreality of the mere present that is found in Thomas Hardy's novels and even more in his poems. One is conscious of this all along the Dorset coast with its dramatic sequence of crag and cavern. It has no counterpart in England. No other county has anything like Chesil Bank, for example. Every reader who knows his Dorset must have had experiences of this omnipresence of the past in the county. I remember sensing it almost overwhelmingly thirty years ago as I stood on the great headland of Purbeck. On nearly every ridge prehistoric earthworks are found. Some of the people who constructed these must have lived in the valleys.

The hill-tops could not have sustained them. So even what we now regard as the Saxon landscape of the vales, the man-made landscape of Dorset, must in fact be immensely old. The Romano-British had tamed the land long before the Saxons arrived. Hambledon Hill near Blandford Forum, hardly less than Maiden Castle at Dorchester, gives some idea of the scale of this early occupation upon which the Saxon scene was to be superimposed. So the landscape of Dorset, almost equally with their personal genius, must have contributed to the spell that continues to be cast on their readers by William Barnes and Thomas Hardy. Even the speech has an individuality that is as authentically derived from the West Saxons as that of the North East is from the Vikings. Most marked is the substitution of *z* for *s* in such words as those that repeat themselves so often in the poems of William Barnes, whose descriptions of the north-west of the county, particularly of the vale of Blackmore, sum up so imperishably the essential character of the Dorset so loved by all who know it, the Dorset where

> The zwellen downs, wi' chalky tracks
> A-climmen up their zunny backs,
> Do hide green meads an zedgy brooks,
> An' clumps o' trees wi' glossy rooks,
> an' hearty vo'k to laugh an' zing,
> An' parish-churches in a string
> Wi' tow'rs o' merry bells to ring,
> An' white roads up athirt the hills.

CHAPTER THREE

South West England

SOMERSET · DEVON · CORNWALL

St Matthew's Fair at Bridgwater is celebrated in an old song, with a string of place-names that are as evocative as the personal names in the Widdecombe Fair song:

> The lads and lasses they come through
> From Stowey, Stogursey, Cannington too,
> The farmer from Tidlington, true as my life,
> He's come to the fair to look for a wife.
> O Master John; do you beware,
> Don't go kissing the girls at Bridgwater Fair.

Each of these names had a meaning originally that no-one would suspect to-day if scholars had not gone back to its first appearance. Stowey is not from 'stow', meaning inhabited place or holy place, but from stone, telling us that Nether and Over Stowey were so called because they were villages on a paved road along the deeply wooded Quantocks. Stogursey was the 'stoke' of William de Cursi, or Courcy, who took his name from a town in Normandy. It is one of many places in Somerset with a French derivation. Cannington is the -ton on the Quantock hills.

Even the innocent looking final 'ey' needs to be looked at more carefully in the lowlands of Somerset than in most places. Inland from Bridgwater is the long narrow peninsula of the Polden ridge, with Sedgemoor, 'the marsh where the sedge grew', on one side, Avalon on the other; and with Somerton at the break in the ridge, before it comes back in horse-shoe formation to break again at Langport. We are at the very heart of Somerset here. The county takes its name from Somerton, the headquarters of the Somersaetas, 'the summer dwellers', the people who got their livelihood in low-lying land that was liable to flood in winter, while Langport was important in Saxon times because the river Parrett was navigable to that point. All round the ridge are villages with names that afford clues to the remote past of this fascinating region. The 'Pol' in Polden is plural. The correct form of the name is Poholt, in which the second part stands for 'wood'. So the Poldens were wooded hills by pools. That is to say, they were islands among the flooded marshes. At Domesday, Meare had ten fishermen and three fisheries.

A score or more of village names tell their own story. Several on the Avalon side had holy wells. Chilton, Edington, Polden and Shapwick were among the most renowned. Pedwell, near Ashcott, is probably a corruption of St. Peter's well. The villages on the Sedgemoor side tend to be smaller. Their special interest is that they belonged to the *sowi*, in which 'sow' means stream and 'i' stands for island. Middlezoy and Weston Zoyland, in which we have the West-country substitution of 'z' for 's', were sowi villages. The so-called Lake Villages of Somerset were built by Iron Age people, which again gives special interest to this part of Somerset. So while the county has its hills and valleys, which are among the most beautiful in England, the Somerset of the 'summer dwellers' is unique.

The whole of this watery region is a land of legend and mystery. According to one legend, Joseph of Arimathea made his way over Wirrall (Weary Hill) near Street to reach Glastonbury and there planted in the ground the staff that grew and blossomed as the Holy Thorn. There is not even a fragment of truth in the legend; but this 'cock-and-bull' story invented by the monks to fill the coffers of their abbey fooled generations of pilgrims. Although we temporarily left all traces of heathenism in place-names behind us when we crossed over into Somerset, we came into a land flowing with the milk and honey of Christian superstition. No doubt the eerie character of the countryside contributed to this exceptional gullibility, and it may not be entirely fanciful to suspect Irish blarney. Beckery, near Glastonbury, is derived from *Bec Erin*, meaning 'little Ireland', suggesting that there was a colony of Irish monks at Glastonbury. William of Malmesbury, who never mentioned Joseph of Arimathea or said one word about the King Arthur romance, wrote of Athelney, 'the island of princes', that it was 'not an island in the sea, but so inaccessible on account of bogs and inundation of lakes that it cannot be approached but by boat'.

Another distinctive feature of the region is that so many of the cottages are built of mud, giving the villages a character entirely different from that of the Mendip and the Quantock villages, and one that in less affluent days would make them look like survivals from a vanished culture. Now, of course, such cottages are eagerly sought after and romanticised, particularly in south Devon and National Trust villages like Selworthy and others in the group on the Somerset side of Exmoor.

The three keys to unlock the mysteries of the Somerset Levels are in the abbeys of Muchelney, Glastonbury and Athelney. The 'ey' ending we have discussed, the 'bury' ending is significant in several places as indicative of ancient defences. But for the moment the significance of these three abbeys is that they owned vast expanses of the Somerset lowlands and provide the answers to many place-name questions. Muchelney, once an isolated stronghold surrounded by bogs and streams was founded by King Ine early in the eighth century, Athelney by King Alfred in 878. According to legend. Alfred hid from the Danes in a herdsman's hut on the Isle of Athelney, and when he overcame the Danes showed his gratitude by appointing the herdsman Bishop of Winchester. Both Glastonbury (also founded by King Ine) and Muchelney were rebuilt in Norman times, following an earlier rebuilding of Muchelney by Athelstan as an act of repentance for having executed his brother Edwin.

Turning from the Somerset of piety and superstition to the practical and factual Somerset, we pick up the trail of Vespasian, who led the second Augustan legion into the West Country to reach the lead mines of the Mendips. His eagerness to reach them is shown in the discovery of 'pigs' of lead bearing the stamp of the legionaries at Charterhouse, Somerset, dated 49 AD,which is only six years after the invasion of Kent. The baths at Bath are paved with Mendip lead. To reach the Mendips, Vespasian would pass the grave mounds of chieftains buried nearly two thousand years before his landing. All along the border of Wiltshire with Somerset is a stretch of country pockmarked with the sites of ancient battles and the earthworks of forgotten tribes. The great barrier for centuries would be Selwood Forest, which extended from Malmesbury to Wincanton, a sort of no man's land at the extremity of the West Saxon kingdom, and for centuries the dividing block between the old dioceses of Winchester and Sherborne.

Taking topographical features and documentary records into consideration together, it seems probable that the battle of 658, at which Cenwalh, king of the West Saxons, drove the Britons as far as the Parrett, was the decisive victory that started the real breakthrough of the Saxons into east Somerset. Cenwalh had advanced up the country east of the Severn after the victory over the three kings that gave him control of Gloucester, Cirencester, and Bath, which had enabled the Saxons to cut off the Celts of Wales from those of the western counties of England. We have evidence of this in the strongly Saxon character of the place-names between the Bristol Avon and Taunton. The breach made in the Cotswolds by the Bristol Avon, although circuitous, provided a route to both Bath and the heart of Somerset, although the second part of the breakthrough was long delayed. It took a hundred years to get the forty miles between Bath and Taunton settled. And while these lowlands were being occupied, the Cymri remained undisturbed in the Quantocks, and across the Tone and Parrett, until other West Saxons came up from the Dorset coast after landing at Bridport and Lyme Regis. The Mendips derive the first part of the their name from the Welsh *mynydd*, 'hill'. But why the 'dip'? Could it be 'hop' for valley – the ravine that splits the hills into two parts in Cheddar Gorge? This is so dramatic a natural feature that it could have been transferred to the hills themselves. They would then be the hills of the gorge, just as Pennyghent in Yorkshire is 'the hill of the open country'.

As found elsewhere, the Celts took to the hills when threatened on the Somerset plains, especially where they had got their living by hunting and fishing and not, like the Saxons, by land cultivation. Bindon, quiet enough today, was the scene of the battle that broke the defences of the West and led to the resettlement of the land between the Axe and the Otter. The record of this drive is to be read in the number of place-names, many of them farms, ending in hay, hayes, or hayne, from *haeg*, an enclosure, and in such town and village names as Colyton, Otterton, Sidbury, Ottery and Axmouth, where they found a Romano-British settlement.

The two forces – one from the south, the other from the north – met eventually and started the long history of fruitful settlement in the fertile vale of Taunton Deane. So productive was this central region of Somerset that it reached a peak of prosperity under the Normans.

Even Ilchester, which began as a Roman military station on the Fosse Way, became most important after the Conquest. This phase in the county's history is well documented in place-names. Of the seven hundred English villages bearing a Roman surname, seventy-eight are in Somerset. Professor Tait celebrated this superbly in a single sentence: 'Bagpuise, Bowells, Bubb, Coggles, Crubb, Goose, Gubbals, Puddock,

Pudding and Wallop rub shoulders with Champflower, Courtenay, Curzon, D'Evercy, Lancelyn, Longueville, Monchensie, Montague, Morieux, St. Quentin and Seymour.' The combination of British and Norman names which is so common in the West supports the belief that the people of these parts put up little resistance to the invaders, but settled down peacefully with them to enjoy the plenty that the land provided.

In view of the fertility of Somerset and Devon, it may surprise those who regard the West country as the national playground to hear it said that they are not 'village counties' in the sense that so many in the Midlands and the East are. There are few villages anywhere in England that surpass in beauty those on the old Acland estate, now the property of the National Trust; but these were Acland creations to a degree that only a handful of visitors appreciate. At the valuation of the forests of Somerset made in 1289, North Petherton and Selwood produced revenues from the sale of wood and the letting of pasturage for pigs; Exmoor was a barren waste.

In the reign of James I the Kite Oak was stated to be the only tree of any size on the Moor. Then why, it may be asked, are there so many tree names on Exmoor? The answer is that it was the very barrenness of the landscape that gave such prominence to single trees. So the rounded hill at the head of Chalk Water is called Kittuck after the same Kite Oak that once grew there, and the oak must have got its name because a kite nested in it. Similarly, Withy Bog got its name from a solitary withy. The magnificent woodlands round Porlock were planted by the Aclands. One Sir Thomas alone planted eight hundred thousand. This bareness of Exmoor is reflected in the place-names including 'Mol', which is *moel*, the Welsh word for bare that we get in Malvern, Worcestershire.

The Forest of Exmoor, the Blackdown Hills and the old Forest of Neroche, a corruption of a name meaning 'where the hunting dogs were kept', long separated Devon from Somerset in the north. There is no natural barrier separating Devon from Dorset in the south, so the main infiltration was on that side. This is borne out by the number of place-names of comparatively early date in this part of Devon, and the lack of firm evidence as to the precise line which the eastern boundary of the county followed. But the lack of names ending in -ing or -ingas makes it unlikely that settlement was established even here before the last quarter of the seventh century. There are no pre-Christian burial grounds in Somerset.

If we plot the place-names for evidence with which to date settlement we get a confused picture. Galford in Lew Trenchard – Baring-Gould's parish – was the scene of a battle probably fought between the men of Devon and the men of Cornwall in the eighth century. The Dart valley appears to have been fully occupied by the Saxons in the ninth century. When we get nearer Dartmoor, however, Saxon settlement seems to have been as late as the eleventh century or even later than that.

So we may say that in general the place-names of Devon are predominantly late Saxon until we reach the border with Cornwall, where we find such a name as Clovelly, in which the first element is the Celtic *clawdd*, meaning trench. That progress should have been so slow is not surprising. Invaders who came in from the south were soon up against Dartmoor, which had to be bypassed. It is not surprising, therefore, that this inhospitable land long continued to be sparsely populated except in the valleys, and even in these we find -ton endings rather than -ings or hams. There were, however, Celtic elements in the Exmoor foothills. Charles, north of South Molton in the valley of the Bray, is *carn*, 'rock', *les*, 'court or palace', which must mean that this was the dwelling place of a British chieftain. A Celtic element, *mor-cet*, may survive in Morchard Bishop according to scholars, the 'Mor' being the Welsh *mawr* 'great', and the 'chard' the Welsh *coed* 'wood'. Alternatively, we may think the name is derived from orchard and means no more than that the Bishop grew fruit there! Between the south-western fringes of Dartmoor and the Tamar there are several place-names that are clearly Celtic. The 'Wal' in Walreddon is from *Wealas*. East Wallabrook and West Wallabrook contain the same element and mean 'the Welshman's brook', and it has been suggested that the 'Yell' in some of the farm names, such as Yellaton, Yelland, and Yellowmead is derived from 'ye olde land' and indicates land already cultivated when the Saxons arrived. Scholars, however, look more favourably on such derivations as 'yeld' from elder, and from the Old English *gield*, 'payment, tribute, tax' as we have it in such names as Great and Little Yeldham in Essex.

The resistance of the Celts is shown most conclusively in church dedications. This is most pronounced, as we shall see, in Cornwall. Lady Fox tells us that of the two hundred and twelve ancient churches in Cornwall, one hundred and seventy-four are dedicated to a western saint. But there are as many as fifty in Devon. St. Congar, who is believed to have been buried at Congresbury in Somerset, turns up again in Badgworth, near Axebridge. We have St. Dubricious at Porlock, St. Decuman at Watchet,

St Petroc at Timberscombe and St Benno at Culbone. All these indicate that in those early centuries Christianity was interpreted as an aspect of Celtic nationalism. The Celts regarded themselves then, as so many still do, as God's chosen people, and in the middle of the seventh century Devon was still a Celtic kingdom.

Barnstaple, a chartered town since 930 and the site of a mint, is an apparently simple name that experts will argue about for ever. For us the interest is in the use of the word 'staple' for market instead of 'chipping' as we have it in the Midlands and the East of England. In Chipstable, Somerset, we might be thought to have both, but there the first element is a personal name. At Barnstaple the market may have developed round a staple, or post; but here again we come up against French influence suggesting a body of wool merchants enjoying exclusive privileges – merchants of the staple. And incidentally, among the woodlands east of Barnstaple is Acland Barton, in which the first part is Acca's land. This was the first identified home of the great Acland family, barton being a common West Country word for a yeoman's dwelling. Many of these Bartons were originally granges belonging to monasteries.

In general, the place-names of north Devon and north-west Cornwall suggest that these areas were colonised from West Somerset. The settlers must have kept to the coastal fringe and the Exmoor valleys as they crossed into Devon, where they left their mark in such names as Oare, Culbone, Porlock, Luccombe, Challacombe, Cutcombe, Exford, Winsford and Dulverton.

In the south of Devon the social development of the region is more clearly documented in place-names, especially inland from the Exe. Exeter, the Roman *Isca Dumnoniorum*, occupies the site of the tribal capital of the Dumnonii, just as Winchester occupies the site of the tribal capital of the Belgae, and the Roman plan remains in the main streets. North, High, South and Fore. 'Clyst', a British river name related to the Roman *cluo* 'to wash', is found in several place-names nearby, and is an illustration of the Somerset and Devon habit of substituting 'y' for 'u'. A Saxon abbey was founded in 680, and the rich agricultural land extending from Totnes. 'Tottie's headland', to Prawle Point is still called the South Hams, with the characteristic that so many towns, like Modbury, cling to the hillsides.

Before the Romans came, the mineral wealth of this part of Devon was already being exploited. Tavistock, Ashburton, Chagford and Plympton, the four stannary towns of Devon, take their title from the Latin *stannum*, meaning tin; but they are much older than this proves. As stannary towns they enjoyed the privilege of holding courts under a charter granted by Edward I, and of setting their seal on the tin that was weighed there. Although little more than a village now, Plympton is the mother town of Plymouth. The stannary prison was at Lydford, where the forest courts of Dartmoor were held and administered, according to tradition, in the principle of 'first hang and draw, then hear the case'. The street plan of Lydford still preserves the plan of late Saxon settlements.

Although the Saxons settled the fertile valleys of South Devon from the Axe, the Otter, the Teign, and the Exe so rapidly and so profitably, they did not arrive during the -ing and -ham periods. Most of the names end in -ton, and this late settlement enabled Celtic traditions and superstitions to survive into periods in which they would have been lost in the south-east of England. At Henbury Hill between Honiton and Cullompton concentric ditches of prehistoric fortifications are still to be seen, which would continue in use against the Saxons. At Awliscombe, as at Abbotsbury in Dorset, women long continued to touch secretly a stone in the church wall, as in other places they would touch the phallic symbol of a monolith as a fertility rite.

The Saxons were not in possession of Exeter until about 690. The -ing endings in Devon generally are compounded and not earlier than the eighth century. The advance through the Culme valley gap led to settlements at Hemyock, Uffculme, Cullumpton, Sampford and Tiverton, 'the town of two fords', and at the same time Crediton and Cheriton were being established in the Creedy valley. Several names in the Exe valley indicated later settlement after the woodland had been cleared. These are Stoodleigh, Calverleigh, Withleigh, Cadeleigh, and Stockleigh Pomery, which takes its name from Henry de la Pomeraye, one of the Norman Pomeroys, or Pomerayes, who held vast estates in Devon.

When the Danes landed from their longships in Torbay in 851 and made their way, looting and pillaging in true Viking style across the royal manor of Paignton, the Saxons put up a valiant defence. But in 876 the Danes stormed Exeter and in 878 there was a ferocious battle at Countisbury on the north Devon coast. Scholars argue about the actual site, but this battle appears to have been decisive. Twelve hundred Danes are said to have been slain, with the result that few Scandinavian place-names appear on the county map, either north or south, with the exception of a group in the South Hams, which appears to indicate a successful raid of later date, possibly of the eleventh century.

By Domesday much of Devon must have enjoyed three hundred years of Saxon prosperity. There were still many isolated farmsteads, as there are today for that matter; but sizeable villages had developed, and the Normans lost little time in organising the land as they had done in Somerset and Dorset. The place-names bordering those counties tell their own story. But there are curious differences to be noted, among them the absence in the south of names ending in -cott and -worthy. The most interesting survival from Normanisation is in the many Bucklands found in this region. This does not usually indicate places where the bucks were numerous, or where the beeches (*boc*) grew. In Devon and Somerset it usually means land held under book, or charter, granted by such feudal lords as the Courtenay earls of Devon, who had their headquarters at Tiverton, the Pomeroys and Peverells, the counterparts of the Norman lords we noted in the counties to the east. Buckland was charter land as distinct from folkland or common land. Many of the charters were granted by the abbeys, by this time becoming rich on Devon's fertile soil. Minchin Buckland in Somerset was held from a nunnery, Minchin being from the Old English *mynecen* 'nun'. Buckland Monachorum was the seat of an abbey.

An associated name is Galmpton, found four times in Devon and twice in Somerset (Galhampton and Galmington), a name found nowhere else in England which means the -ton of rent-paying peasants. This suggests that there was a system of land tenure in the West Country that was peculiar to that region. Certainly the social development of the area was rapid between the middle of the twelfth and the middle of the fourteenth centuries, the period in which many of the towns were established and in which the foundations were laid for the prosperity of Devon in the Middle Ages.

Turning to the far West, modern research may have established more links between the place-names on the Devon bank of the Tamar and those on the Cornish bank than were formerly thought to exist, but Cornwall remains a land apart. Its own Celtic language survived until the eighteenth century, whereas Devon was fully Anglicised by the end of the eleventh. Not that this constitutes disloyalty to the English Crown. Far from it. The eldest son of the Sovereign is by custom created Prince of Wales, but he is born Duke of Cornwall and endowed with lands to support the title.

The landscape of Cornwall reiterates both the detachment and the price. There are places where it becomes almost lunar in its outcrops of granite that defy cultivation, and in its white heaps of waste that look more like eruptions than deposits. After the lush combes of Devon the sterility of much of Cornwall sends a shudder through the veins until we reach the coast and feel our spirits rise as we stand in awe before the rugged beauty of mighty rocks. We do not marvel that Penzance is *Pen sans*, the holy headland. And even inland our natural reaction to the strange appearance of the industrialised landscape is modified when we learn or reflect that the fame of the Cornish tin mines extended east to Phoenicia, and that they are mentioned in the fourth century BC by a traveller from the East called Pytheas. Brown Willy is a corruption of *Bryn Huel*, the tin mine ridge. The stannary court of the Duchy of Cornwall is believed to have been a continuation of an ancient Celtic court held on the summit of Crokern Tor, where concentric seats are cut in the rock.

The 'combes' and 'tors' of Devon disappear as we move into the heart of Cornwall, to be replaced by 'nans' for valleys and 'carrs' or 'bres' for cairns or piles of rock. The kinship is with Wales, where 'nan' becomes 'nant' and 'carr' becomes 'caer'. There are many other parallels. Church is 'eglwys' in Wales, 'eglos' in Cornwall. 'Maen' for stone in Wales is 'men' in Cornwall. Helbron combines *heyle*, estuary and *bron*, hill. Pen is found in both for hill or headland. So it comes about that:

> By Tre, Ros, Car, Lan, Pol and Pen
> You well may know all Cornish men.

'Tre' is derived from the Celtic *tref* or *trev*, meaning a farmstead or later a hamlet, 'ros' means heath, 'lan' a church, 'pol', as we saw in Somerset, pool or stream. Tregear and Tregair are homesteads near a *caer*, or fort. Tremaine is the hamlet of the *maen*, or stone, which suggests that the hill settlement came first. In Tremorton, the Saxon -ton is added to the Celtic root.

We are assured that there are more than a thousand compounds of 'tre' in Cornwall. But to anyone coming in from the east or north of England, Cornwall seems to be full of strange-sounding names that slip off the tongue like incantations. What can we make at first sight of such names as Marazion, Menabilly, Nanjizal, Zelah or Mevagissey?

So as we travel to the extreme West we find increasing evidence of the imaginative nature of the Celt, which is so different from the earthy practicality of the Saxon. Superstition even finds expression in the round houses that we are told were so built to provide no corner for the Devil to hide in. I don't recall coming across that explanation for the round towers of East Anglia! But whatever truth there may be in this, Cornwall incontestably has the distinction of having produced the earliest architecture in England in its chambered tombs, called quoits, most of which are on ridges overlooking the sea, although Trethevy Quoit is on the southern edge of Bodmin Moor. John Norden described it as 'a little howse raysed of mightie stones, standing on a little hill within a feilde'. Other old antiquaries described these Stone Age tombs as 'Druids' Altars'. The greatest concentration of megalithic tombs is along the northern heights of the Penwith moors: Zennor Quoit, Mulfra Quoit, Chun Quoit, Lanyon Quoit, West Lanyon Quoit, and Menm-an-Tol, 'the stone with the hole', known locally as the Crick Stone because people would crawl through the hole to relieve cricks in their back, and children would be put through the hole nine times against the sun as a cure for rickets. Stones with holes in them seem to have been regarded with veneration in many places, perhaps as representations of the womb in a mother-goddess cult.

Old customs survive in Cornwall as in no other part of England. Helston has the Furry Dance, Towednack the Cuckoo Feast, Padstow the hobby-horse, St. Hilary a Christmas miracle play, St. Madron's Well the bent-pin ceremony on Holy Thursday and St. Ives two ancient customs. There are about a hundred holy wells in Cornwall, and the presence of an ancient cross is indicated by the occurrence of 'crowse' or 'grouse' in the place-name; but here again superstition crept in. Near St. Buryan there is a place called Crowz-an-Wragh, which means the witch's cross.

The 'z' in this place-name, which is found again in Zennor, (derived from Senara, the name of a woman saint) reminds us of the many substitutions of 'z' for 's' in Dorset.

The north-east of Cornwall is another region of Arthurian romance. Camelford is identified with Camelot, and Slaughter Bridge is alleged to have been the scene of Arthur's final battle. At Tintagel the plot thickens with Merlin's Cave being pointed out below Arthur's Castle and Dozmary Pool as the lake into which the sword Excalibur was thrown.

When we turn from scenes of romance to scenes of sanctity Cornwall becomes even more impressive. Unfortunately most of the lives of the saints were destroyed at the Dissolution of the monasteries, although Leland noted in his *Itinerary* that he had seen some of them. The life of St. Ia, who gave her name to St. Ives, was one. Among Irish saints whose names are commemorated in Cornish place-names are Buriena, Levan,

Sennen and Just. These were as much revered in wells and springs as in churches. Others are associated with stones. St Piran became the patron saint of the Cornish tin miners, and was said to have arrived from Ireland on a mill-stone. Other saints came from Wales. The most famous being St Petroc, son of a Welsh king, who landed on the bank of the Camel. One historian of Cornwall, Charles Henderson, tells us that ninety-eight of the two hundred and fifty four Cornish parishes originated in monastic foundations.

Even the phlegmatic Saxons continued the mystic traditions of Cornwall in that it was under them that the first stone crosses were set up. They can still be seen in every part of the county, although they were certainly not expressions of Saxon culture. There are hundreds of them in the far west. Most are wheel-headed.

The survival of so much Celtic culture in Cornwall is to some extent explained by the fact that contrary to their normal practice the Romans did not re-open the tin mines and reorganise the county immediately on arrival. At the time of the Roman occupation much of the Cornish tin trade had been lost to north-west Spain. There was even less for the Romans to go for in Cornwall than there had been in east Devon, where the three Roman villas discovered are near the Dorset border. So Exeter remained the most westerly town to come under Roman control. In the later years of the occupation the delay was remedied and a few brave spirits did reach Cornwall to build a small enclosure at Tregear, two miles west of Bodmin, which now appears on the map as Campfield, and another group may have fortified a small rectangular enclosure at Bosence. These suggest that eventually a small amount of tin was mined by the Romans and exported from the Helford River. But nothing so far discovered suggests more than small-scale and possibly experimental working during the early period of the Roman occupation, and when they did show interest it was not through direct intervention. The large number of Roman coins of the third and fourth centuries found in Cornwall suggests that even then the tin was worked by the natives and bought from them by Roman officials. This would be consistent with the discovery of a villa on the Roman model at Magor, between Camborne and the coast, and with the existence of short lengths of paved roads and two milestones, one at St Hilary and one at Breage, which indicate that there was a road of some kind to Porthleven from the direction of St Michael's Mount. Probably, a main factor in the lack of evidence for Roman occupation in Cornwall is that its resources were inadequate to form the basis for the urban way of life that the Romans cultivated.

Even the Saxons, who were not urban-minded, required more amenities than the Celts, whose early settlements were on hill-tops, and who were hunters rather than tillers of the soil. When the population did increase, whether before or after the Saxon infiltration, the first shortage in these hill-top settlements would be water. It may well have been this need for water that led to the superstitious regard for wells, each of which in course of time became dedicated to a saint or benevolent spirit. To the Saxons the need for water was crucial, so in Cornwall as everywhere else their axes were swung and their ploughs driven through the reluctant soil. The vigour of this onslaught is described in the Life of St Brioc: 'All', we read, 'gird themselves to work, they cut down trees, root up bushes, tear up brambles and tangled thorns, and soon convert a dense wood into a clearing.' It is in these places that a Saxon terminal, usually -ton, is added to a Celtic name. We have examples in Binnerton, Callington, Winnianton and Helston. By plotting them we see the lines of the Saxon advance, which as elsewhere was from the rivers; but the number of names on the map indicating isolated Celtic farmsteads (tres) and abodes (bods) suggests that when the Saxons came the Celts withdrew here in the manner characteristic of them over the whole of western England: that is to say, into small settlements in the hills, where they could continue to live the free independent life that makes the Celt the devil-may-care character he always was and always will be.

CHAPTER FOUR

The West Midlands

GLOUCESTERSHIRE · WORCESTERSHIRE
HEREFORDSHIRE · SHROPSHIRE

When the West Saxons captured Gloucester they became possessors of a
prosperous region strewn with the sites of Roman villas. They had sailed
up the Coln from the Thames Valley to settle at Fairford, Bibury and
Chedworth, where the most complete surviving relic of the Roman occupation is to be seen along with the site of a Roman temple half a mile
away. Their earliest villages included Avening, named after the river,
and Arlingham, 'the homestead of the earl's people'. The Angles came
into the county shortly afterwards to establish villages at Beckford and
Ebrington, and after the victory of Penda of Mercia over the West Saxons at Cirencester in 628 the Angles and Saxons combined to found a
new kingdom, the kingdom of Hwicce, which covered the whole of
Gloucestershire east of the Severn, most of Worcestershire and West
Warwickshire.

The Mercian king, Coenwulf, founded a monastery at Winchcombe
about 798, and this in course of time came to be as important to the north
Cotswolds as Gloucester was to the south. In fact, in the ninth century it
formed a separate province and remained one until about 1017. In the
south west there was Cirencester on the river Churn, which had been the
fort of the Cornovii, a tribe so powerful that earthworks at nearby
Bagendon have been compared with those at Colchester and St Albans.
Cirencester's regnal name was modified into the Old English, *Ciern* and
Cyrn, to which the name of a Roman station was added; but the form in
which we have it today was the result of feudal influence which is found
impressively throughout the West Midlands. Not least among the
imposing memorials to Norman power still standing are the great tithe
barns built by heads of wealthy abbeys. One is to be seen at Frocester,
the Roman station on the river Frome, whose name is commonly shor-

tened to Froster, just as Cirencester's is to Sisiter. Another great tithe barn stands at Stanway (paved road). This was built by the Abbot of Tewkesbury, only one of the many powerful clerics of this fertile region. At Domesday the largest landowners in the county were the cathedral church at Worcester and the abbeys at Winchcombe, Evesham and Gloucester.

This later prosperity is so firmly implanted in the Cotswold landscape as we see it now, that earlier cultures tend to appear legendary. We have an example of this in a passage in Camden's *Britannia*, where we read of the dwindled hamlet of Dorn in the village of Blockley near Chipping Camden: 'The country people have a tradition that Dorn was formerly a city, and many old foundations that have been dug up there with an abundance of Roman and British coins commonly found by the husbandmen, and the lines in which the streets ran being still very discernible . . . show that a colony of Romans must have resided here.'

Blockley is in a valley. On the hilltops there are many ancient earthworks built as animal stockades. We find them at Painswick, another Normanised name, famous for the yews that gave Uley its name. Above Uley is the great burial mound called Hetty Pegler's Tump; on Cleeve Hill, Belas Knap. Both Tump and Knap are regional names, the one for barrow, the other for top. The highest settlement in Gloucestershire is Stow-on-the-Wold:

> Stow on the Wold,
> Where the wind blows cold.

This hill-top town probably owes its origin to the need for a look-out post on the prehistoric Fosse Way. If we examine the roads and trackways hereabouts we see how Celtic, Roman, and succeeding cultures took advantage of what was already there. Exhibits in the local museum make it plain that Stow had been a Celtic fortress long before the Romans came and it has continued, despite its small size, to figure prominently in each succeeding culture. Two Roman villas have been excavated there, and its present triangular shape is the result of a mediaeval castle dominating it.

The historical significance of Cotswold names continues to raise questions for experts. Is Moreton-in-Marsh, for example, derived from Moreton Henmarsh (wild-bird marsh), as Ekwall says it is, or should the 'marsh' in the name be *marc*, meaning boundary, an alternative suggested by more than one recent authority? The alternative is inspired by the fact that two miles east is the Four Shires Stone, where formerly the counties of Gloucestershire, Oxfordshire, Warwickshire and Worcestershire met. Now it should be the Three Shires Stone, since Worcestershire drew back long before the recent reorganisation of local government. At Bourton-on-the-Water is Salmonsbury Camp, sixty acres enclosed by tall ramparts to provide a place of safety when the tribesmen were at war, suggesting that Bourton is as ancient as Stow.

Many Cotswold villages and small towns owe much of their attraction to their names. But not all. The Swells and the Slaughters are not engagingly named, but they can provide evidence of continuous occupation since Neolithic times. The name Swell is derived from an Old English word for 'spring', Slaughter from one meaning 'slough', suggesting a muddy place. Oddly enough, this word appears in no other English place-name; but a similar element is found in German place-names. Sapperton, by contrast, means what it appears to mean. It is the ton of the soapmakers.

Despite so many ancient sites in this part of Gloucestershire, and evidence that as early as the third century cloaks woven from the wool of Cotswold sheep were included in a list of exports from Britain mentioned in an edict of Diocletian, there were few pre-Saxon settlements of any size north of Gloucester. Collingwood and Myers, in *Roman Britain and the English Settlements*, tell us that in Roman times 'the triangle whose corners lie at Gloucester, Lincoln, and Chester' was the most sparsely inhabited region in Britain. It was clearly the Saxons who created the enduring Cotswold landscape, and it was the wool from their sheep that laid the foundation of all the wealth that followed. Much of this was the result of the prudent husbandry of the abbeys. Gloucester had a large flock at Evenlode in the eighth century; Cirencester had already become an important wool market at Domesday. This explains why the plateau was settled before the valleys, which for the most part were heavily wooded, except in such places as Bourton-on-the-Water and Moreton-in-Marsh, where there were gravel beds between streams. The wide streets of the most typical Cotswold towns were the market places into which from their foundation the flocks of the abbots were shepherded for sale. Many incorporate 'Ship' for sheep in their names, frequently followed by that of their Norman lord.

While wool is the foundation of Gloucester's fame, it must not be forgotten that the county has another industrial tradition. The Forest of Dean was being mined for iron-ore in the first century, and a third-century mine at Lydney has shown that the methods employed then were far from primitive. The industry gave the county such names as Cinderford and Coleford, places where the charcoal was produced for smelting.

It was the main characteristic of the shires that they were centred on major military sites which became county towns. These came at the end of the Danish invasions which culminated in Cnut's succession to the English throne in 1016. It was certainly at this time that Gloucester became the capital of a new and enlarged shire. In the neighbouring county of Worcestershire a different tradition led up to the establishment of ordered government. This is reflected in the county's place-names, and not least in that of the county itself. Worcester is 'the Roman fort of the tribe called *Wigoran* or Weogoran', a tribal name that was modified in the name of Wyre Forest, and may be from the British river name found in Lancashire, where it means 'winding river'. Wyre Forest in the ninth century covered a vast area on the western bank of the Severn and extended for miles north-west of Worcester. The significance of the city's name is that the Romans saw that the Severn must be the boundary to be defended valiantly aginst the Britons. Defensive earthworks are numerous on the west bank. From these the Romans drove the Britons towards Wales, while they established for themselves a well-defended region to the east by erecting forts from the Avon to the Severn.

Above the valley rise the Malvern Hills, a massive range nine miles long capped by one of the most magnificent Iron Age camps in England. To these hills tribesmen retreated when invasion threatened, and anyone who stands on the top of the British camp and looks across Herefordshire towards the Welsh mountains can appreciate the problem that faced the Romans when they asked themselves how the rich valleys of Gloucestershire were to be protected. If the Celts could hold out so long on the Quantocks, how much longer they would be able to hold out on the Malverns. We shall see how the Normans solved the problem when we look at Herefordshire; but here in Worcestershire the defensive position of the Malverns had to be seen in relation to two other British camps east of the Severn, both superb look-out stations. One is at Wychbury, 'the fortified camp of the Hwicce', situated above Pedmore and Hagley to command a view of the Stour valley, the other is at Bredon, a name containing the Welsh *bre* for hill, overlooking the Severn and Avon valleys.

Several Celtic names in the Malvern foothills and in the hill itself,

which means 'bare hill' from the Welsh elements *moel* and *bryn*, are conclusive evidence of British survival. Minor Celtic names are the Wych at
West Malvern, Pendock, meaning 'the hill where the barley grows',
Pengethly, the head of the *celli*, which means wood, and Mathon, tucked
into the hills below West Malvern, mysteriously meaning 'treasure' or
'gift'. To the north is Storridge, which means 'stony ridge'.

These Celtic names confirm what we know from other sources, that as
a region for settlement Worcestershire did not greatly attract the
Romans. They much preferred Gloucestershire. Their roads scarcely
affected the territory of the Hwicce. It is true that the Icknield Way
formed the eastern boundary of what became the new county for a short
distance; but most of the region lay too far to the west of the great military road that ran through Gloucester. Watling Street crossed the Severn
at Wroxeter; the Fosse Way, which means the ditched way, barely
touched the county. As for the value of the territory, they decided that
Worcestershire was too densely wooded for easy occupation, and that
when it was compared with Gloucestershire, there was little to go for.

In the remoter parts the four great forests of Feckenham, Om-
bersley, Horewell and Malvern had a traditional way of life that
would be resistant to change, and the same could be said of the Severn
marshes which would continue to be constantly under threat from the
Britons, especially from the camp in the Malvern Hills. So the Romans
appear to have decided that as so little was to be gained by conquest,
there was no point in disturbing the British, provided they could be held
in check from Worcester, and so long as the salt from Droitwich could be
made available in adequate quantity.

One result of the great value of the salt from Droitwich was a veritable
web of saltways threading their way in all directions from its ancient
mines. As late as the Middle Ages, Droitwich was the only considerable
district in the Midlands producing this valuable commodity, which was
carried along roads and hillside tracks by packhorses. The chief of these
saltways were the Upper and Lower. The Upper ran north from Droitwich to join the Icknield Way south of Birmingham and thence south to
Worcester, Tewkesbury and Gloucester. The Lower Saltway ran from
Droitwich through Feckenham and Alcester to Stratford-on-Avon.
Domesday Book shows that thirty-six vills (townships) in Worcestershire had salt rights in Droitwich, along with ten each in Gloucestershire and Herefordshire, six in Warwickshire, two in Oxfordshire and
one in Buckinghamshire. 'Salt' in any place-name, therefore, is impor-

tant. We get it at Salt in Staffordshire, Salterford in Nottinghamshire, Salterton in Devon; but the 'Sal' in the Salwarpe River in Worcestershire is not from salt but from sallow.

The lack of interest taken by the Romans in Worcestershire meant that after the withdrawal it was possible for the strong tribe of the Hwicce to occupy the entire region, with their king, or under-king, reigning from Worcester. In 679 the bishop of the tribe made this ancient tribal capital the head of his See, and as it was from this permanent foundation that the modern county grew it is not surprising that its life-style has always been ecclesiastical rather than martial, although it has to be admitted that some of its monastic houses had their origins in alleged events that must appear to us now to be fanciful rather than factual. Evesham, for example, founded in 709, is said to have come into being as the result of a herdsman named Eoves recounting to the bishop how, while tending his swine in the forest of the bank of the Avon, a beautiful lady, with an appearance brighter than the sun, came towards him singing heavenly songs. As this could be no other than the Virgin, a monastery was founded where the vision occurred. Other monasteries were founded as near as Fladbury, Pershore and Bredon.

But although Worcestershire was to become as monastic as Gloucestershire was to become baronial and eventually ducal, there was considerable survival of heathenism in the county. The first element in Arrowfield in the north-east is derived from *hearg*, 'sacred grove', and shows that here was a field associated with heathen worship. Another indication of the comparatively late settlement of north Worcestershire is in the number of place-names with feminine personal elements. Alvechurch was the church of a woman. White Ladies Aston was held by the Cistercian nuns of Whitstones.

Wychwood Forest is in Oxfordshire; but it means 'the forest of the Hwicce' and provides a clue to one route followed by the tribe as they moved into north Worcestershire; but we need to be careful about drawing conclusions about the movements of the Hwicce themselves because they assimilated smaller tribes. The Wixna, whose name has been contorted into Whitsun for the small brook that runs between Stratford and Worcester, was one that lost its identity completely, yet the Wixna figure in Lincolnshire, where they were related to the Spaldas. The earliest form of Conderton was Cantuarton, 'the -ton of the Kentishmen', and shows that there was a Kentish settlement below Bredon. Phepson must have derived its name from a mid-Anglian tribe, and there is interesting evidence of Anglian influence in three names containing 'bold' for building. They are Newbold-on-Stour, Wychbold, and Boughton Park, Bedwardine. This element occurs frequently in the north Midlands, but nowhere else so far south. So there were settlers coming in from the north and the east, although obviously most would come from the south and west.

An interesting aspect of these group settlements from other regions is that people were motivated from an early date, comparatively speaking, to penetrate dense natural forest and make a home there. The history of forest clearance from the first to the tenth centuries would make a fascinating study, not least for the evidence it might produce for the survival of ancient customs. Forests have always been places of mystery and superstition, and it is to be noted that many heathen elements are found in the place-names of the triangle north of the confluence of the Severn and the Avon.

The peaceful rule of the region came to an end when the Danes over-ran Mercia; but Ethelred, husband of Ethelfleda, whom we shall meet later, rebuilt the ruined walls of Worcester and again the city came under the beneficent influence of the Church. The great advantage of this ecclesiastical tradition is that Worcestershire is so rich in records preserved by the monks, not all of which inspire confidence in Divine guidance. One of the most fascinating stories in the eleventh-century chronicle of Florence of Worcester is recounted by M. D. Anderson in *History and Imagery in British Churches*. It relates how, at Clent (with its Scandinavian-sounding name) in the hills of the north-east of the county, a miracle occurred. Shortly after Kenelm, while still a child, succeeded his father, King Kenulph of Mercia, he was murdered by Ascobert, the lover of his elder sister Quendreda, who coveted the throne. A rumour was immediately put about by the murderers that the child king had mysteriously disappeared and that the penalty for so much as mentioning his name would be death. This evil design was frustrated when a white dove dropped a scroll before the Pope as he celebrated Mass in St Peter's. On it was written the couplet:

> In Clent, at Cowbach, lieth under a thorn
> His head off-shorn, Kenelm, king-born.

The Pope requested the Archbishop of Canterbury to investigate, and when he did so his searchers were guided to the grave by the lowing of a white cow. There they found a blood-stained knife beside the body, and when they removed it a fountain of pure water gushed forth, which attracted pilgrims from every point of the compass. St Kenelm's church at Clent is built on the site.

In the eleventh century there were enough Scandinavians in the county for a bishop to refer to all the theyns in Worcestershire. Whether this use of the word 'theyn' has been taken too seriously is for scholars to comment on. So far as place-names are concerned we can only note that if they were there in large numbers they have left few traces of their sojourn. This may, however, simply mean that most of the place-names were already fixed before they reached the county.

Having noted the influence of the Normans in neighbouring counties, it is remarkable that so few Normanised names are found in Worcestershire. There is Chaddesley Corbett, in which the surname is from the Old French word for 'raven' and suggests that it was a byname, perhaps for someone with raven hair. A family of that name held the manor from the twelfth century. The 'Lovett' in Elmley Lovett may be similarly disrespectful. It means 'wolf cub'. Broughton Hackett, another not very resounding Norman name, is from a French family. But Worcestershire has one great Norman family figuring in its history in the Beauchamps of Elmley Castle. All this suggests that the major influence of the Normans was through the Benedictines of Worcester, Tewkesbury, Pershore and Evesham, thus continuing the well-established ecclesiastical domination – or paternalism, if a benign view is taken of the county's history – in the Middle Ages.

Although Herefordshire became the diocese of practically the whole of Mercia west of the Severn it could never be thought a predominantly monastic county. Its landscape and economy everywhere reflect a way of life more akin to that of Wales than to that of any other part of England. It is still entirely pastoral. Hereford is its only city. Its five towns, Bromyard, Kington, Leominster, Ross and Ledbury, with their attractive black-and-white timbered buildings, retain much of the character of villages. Their inhabitants are country folk. Welsh-sounding names are everywhere, especially in the west and south of the county. There are Tre-s and Lan-s that twist the tongue like Llanveyno, Llandinabo, and Llangarren. In Pencoyd we have both the Welsh *pen* for hill and *coed* for wood.

In the east of the county the Saxon -ton turns up in Ashton and Yatton; -ham and -ton in Brockhampton; -ing and -wick in Ullingswick; hope in Woolhope; -ley in Putley; -low in Wolferlow. But while it is plain that the Saxons drove the Britons out of the valleys in the east, they never disloged them from the orchard country between the Forest of Dean and Madeley, which means 'good place', from the Welsh *mad* 'good' and *lle* 'place'. Domesday Book confirms this in the note, 'hoc est bonus locus'. This region, which was commemorated in the name of a deanery, was called Archenfield. The etymology of the name appears to be obscure but is surely Welsh, and the same may be said of many Herefordshire place-names about which scholars argue. Eardisland, regarded by many as the county's most beautiful village, has a more complicated construction than might appear. The 'Ear' may be from 'Earl', the 'land' may be from *leon*, an Old English word for district; but equally the first element may be from the river Arrow, a British river name cognate with the Welsh *ariant*, silver. The final element 'land' may be the Welsh *llion*. All we can be sure of is that experts tell us that 'land' in Eardisland, Kingsland and Monksland do not mean anything so obvious as we might suppose, and that when the English bring their influence to bear on the Welsh language the result tends to be regrettable. On the other hand, the English might complain that the Celtic habit of muting voice consonants to breath consonants as in Tintern and Tintagel, where *din* 'hill' becomes 'Tin', doesn't help!

In support of the argument that where alternative derivations are feasible the Welsh one is to be preferred we might note the large number of churches dedicated to Welsh saints, one of whom is the Saint Dubricius we encountered at Porlock in Somerset. The story goes that this bishop of the old Celtic church was born in a fire in which his grandfather, a local king, tried to burn his mother after failing to drown her in the Wye.

After glancing here and there among place-names on the Herefordshire map in the hope of being able to detect a pattern, we come to the name of the county-town itself, the derivation of which is more speculative than that of any other. The 'ford' part is safe enough; but if it had been a Roman ford the name of the town would probably have included 'Street' as we have it in Stretford. It was obviously a ford of great strategic importance to advancing and retreating armies, and one is tempted to speculate on a boundary or hardway origin; but perhaps it would be wiser to escape from a tricky subject by following the example of Thomas Fuller and summing up the county's characteristics in another name entirely. He wrote: 'Besides, this Shire better answereth (as to the sound thereof) the name of Pomerania than the dukedom of Germany so called, being a continued orchard of apple-trees, whereof much cider is made.' As the Danes were so much more ruthless than the Saxons in taking what they wanted, it is odd that they did not take possession of Herefordshire's rich pastures. Foreign influence became dominant for one purpose only, that of defence.

Watling Street enters the county at Leintwardine, in which 'wardine' is the West Midlands form of Worthy, to pass by Brandon Camp, the Roman Bravium, eventually to reach Kenchester, where it is to be noted that Roman place-names in Herefordshire tend to incorporate 'e' rather than 'a'. So we have Stretford for the commoner Stratford, and Stretton Grandison, between which and Ashperton the Roman road follows the modern highway with the characteristic straightness that is so different from the winding lanes that make up most of the county's road system. Another Roman road crosses the Wye near Eaton Bishop and runs from there to Madeley, where it retains the name of Stone Street, to pass out of the county on its way to Abergavenny, the *Gobannium* of the Romans. Another enters the county from Newent in the south east and runs south of Ross to *Ariconium*.

The Normans clearly saw the region as the base for the conquest of South Wales. So we get the many deserted castles of Herefordshire and Monmouthshire that give such a romantic aspect to the border landscape, and provide clues to the petty kingdoms governed by the 'lords marcher', such as the Lacys of Holme Lacy, the Despensers, the Clares, and above all the Mortimers, who spilt over into Worcestershire. The Clares were at Goodrich on the Wye, the Vaughans at Francis Kilvert's Bredwardine. Wigmore was the great stronghold of the Mortimers. Among other castles were Wilton, Brampton Bryan, Bollitree, Eardisley, Kinnersley, and Ewys Harold, where only the mound and earthworks remain. Many were held as fortresses under the Earl of Hereford, others were look-out posts on small tumps, as mounds and barrows are called in Herefordshire and Gloucestershire. Acton Beauchamp was the -ton by the oaks of the Beauchamp family.

The same defensive pattern continues along the Welsh border of Shropshire, where Iron Age forts crown most of the hills. Of these the hill fort at Old Oswestry is pre-eminent. Sir Cyril Fox described it as 'the outstanding work of the early Iron Age type on the Marches of Wales'. It covers forty acres. Pentresbury might be described as the sun with a group of satellite forts. Offa's Dyke, the great earthwork constructed with immense engineering skill that took advantage of every natural feature of the land, was thrown up about 785 by King Offa of Mercia to keep out the Welsh along the entire line between the mouth of the Dee and the mouth of the Wye. It cannot have been entirely successful in this, because the character of many of the Welsh names found in the Forest of Clun near Oswestry and south of Shrewsbury indicates immigration rather than survival. Oswestry was a Welsh town until comparatively recently. Only gradually did the Welsh language and the Welsh mode of life there give place to the English. Even places fully settled by the English may have been settled later by the Welsh. In the Honour of Clun, the population of Tempitsur, 'The Teme dwellers', was almost entirely Welsh according to Trevor Rowley in *The Shropshire Landscape*. To understand the vagaries of place-name nomenclature in Shropshire it has to be appreciated that the county is a land of lost villages, which only emerged as an administrative unit early in the eleventh century, and of villages that were recorded in the Domesday Book many appear only as farms or small hamlets today. Of the sixty-one hamlets recorded in the Domesday Survey, eight have been deserted and thirty-five survive as isolated farms. As a densely wooded region on the edge of the Welsh mountains its attraction to those who wanted to get their living from the soil was small.

The settlement of this largest of all the inland counties was from the rivers, which is normal; but to a greater degree than with most it was from the Ridgeways, the most important of which was the Clun-Clee. Clun, Clunbury, Clungunford and Clunton all take their names from the river Clun, a British name that has the same origin as the River Colne in Essex. Clee, meaning 'clay', is a range of hills that gave rise to even more place-names, such as Clee St Margaret, Clee Stanton, Cleobury Mortimer and North Cleobury. The incorporation of a Norman element in a Shropshire place-name is held to have been merely to avoid confusion. There were so many Actons and Stantons with nothing to distinguish them that the simple device of adding the name of the Norman owner was adopted. By this means distinctive identity was given to Acton-Burnell, Acton-Pigot, Acton-Reynold and Acton-Scott.

There are many examples of this combining of elements. Neen Sollars and Neen Savage start with a British river name identical with Nene, to which the names of their Norman owners are added.

One of the outstanding features of Shropshire is the size of the parishes created in the eighth and ninth century, some of which were co-extensive with Hundreds. One of the largest, if not the largest, was Much Wenlock, a name derived from the Welsh *gwyn-loc*, 'white church'. As in

Herefordshire, the dedications of the Shropshire churches, many of which were served by group ministries from monastic houses, give clues to origins. A new administrative system was imposed on the Saxon and Celtic population by the bishops in the Middle Ages, but many dedications to Welsh saints bear evidence to earlier settlement. The church at Atcham is dedicated to St Eata, who died in 685, the old church at Cressage to the Welsh St Samson, who died in 565, while in Corvedale a group of Saxon churches survive. Most of the early monasteries were established close to roads or rivers, and the development of the parish system from minster churches provides a clue to the clearing of the forests. At the same time, the potentialities of the region for hunting were recognised by the Norman lords. Hunting lodges were built, land that had been cleared was imparked, and it is interesting to find that these are often given names incorporating 'haye', the word for enclosure that we found so frequently in Dorset, Somerset and Devon. The Forest of Hayes, however, is more likely to be derived from *haes*, meaning brushwood.

The Saxon settlement of Shropshire was late, and the size and character of the hamlets is consistent with that found elsewhere in heavily wooded country. The -hams are to be found in the south, usually associated with a British river name. Corfham, from the River Corve; Caynham, from the River Key, and Lydham, from the River Lyde are examples. In the west of the county there are nine Waltons and four Walcots. These have special significance near the Welsh border. The Saxons were inclined to disparage the Welsh, and the incorporation of 'Wal' or *Walh* into a place-name was not intended to be complimentary. Some of these places continued until recent times to be Welsh-English.

We have moved in this chapter through wealthy Gloucestershire, ecclesiastical Worcestershire, pastoral Herefordshire, into a region that long remained poor. Much was done by the Romans and Normans for its defence and administration, little for its prosperity. The Saxons fared better in other counties. Many of its Norman churches escaped both rebuilding when the wool trade flourished and callous restoration in the nineteenth century. But Shropshire has its glories. Ludlow, 'the hill on the rapid', is one of the finest towns in England, with a magnificent church dedicated to St Lawrence and the castle guarding the confluence of the Teme and the Corve where Milton's *Comus* was first performed before the Earl of Bridgewater, Lord President of Wales, in 1634. The county town, Shrewsbury, splendidly situated on a peninsula within a horseshoe bend of the Severn, was Salopesberia in 1094, from which we get the county's alternative name of Salop. And how fortunate this was for the Normans, who couldn't cope with the intrusive 'R's' of Shropshire!

CHAPTER FIVE

The South Midlands

OXFORDSHIRE · WARWICKSHIRE
NORTHAMPTONSHIRE · HUNTINGDONSHIRE
BEDFORDSHIRE · BUCKINGHAMSHIRE
HERTFORDSHIRE

The Cotswolds spill over into Oxfordshire from Gloucestershire in low limestone hills, separating woodland valleys with villages grouped round river crossings or on rising ground, all built in characteristic cottage style. Judging by the number near streams, with -ford as part of their name, water and communications were the determining factors in selecting most of the sites. Oxford was the ford for oxen, Heyford was probably the ford used at the hay harvest. As usual, honest-to-God Saxon names are ennobled by the surnames of their Norman lords. So Sibba's fords become Sibford Ferris and Sibford Gower. Shillingford amongst these -ford names presents a problem. As it is on the Thames, a ferry with a shilling toll looks cheap but possible until we look up its earliest appearance, and find that a tribal name is suggested which occurs twice in Devonshire, once near Exeter and once in Bampton.

The Oxfordshire bank of the Thames suffered from two disadvantages for early settlement: one topographical, the other racial. It was liable to flood, and in the eighth century it was too close to the territory in dispute between the kingdoms of Wessex and Mercia. Nevertheless, the crossing of the Thames by a Roman road at Dorchester, which had been important since the Bronze Age, and was the seat of the first West Saxon bishopric, brought settlers of both Saxon and Anglian origin. The manor of Bensington, which extended for thirteen miles from Henley to the river Thames, was the Windsor of the early Saxon kings.

The 'Dorc' in Dorchester is from a British word meaning 'bright', which occurs in Surrey in the river that gave Dorking its name.

Few British names have survived in Oxfordshire, and this makes the Wychwoods so interesting. We have already seen how extensive the territory of the Hwicce was, and how influential when the Principality, if

77

such it may be called, was co-extensive with the old diocese of Worcester, which included part of west Oxfordshire. Its limit appears to have been marked by the name Whichford in Warwickshire, seven miles east of Moreton-in-Marsh, and the recurrence of the name in many places containing 'under' shows how extensive Wychwood Forest was. We think of Milton-under-Wychwood, Shipton-under-Wychwood, and Ascot-under-Wychwood in the valley of the Evenlode, so-named from Eowla's passage or ferry. And all, it may be noted, are true to the convention of using the preposition 'under' before the name of the forest in which it stood.

Wychwood was only one of the forests that drew their sustenance from the rich clay of the Oxfordshire valleys. To the east of it lay Woodstock Chase, a favourite hunting ground of Norman kings. The forests of Shotover and Stowood lay to the east of Oxford city – Stowood meaning 'stone wood', Shotover 'hill with a steep slope', a fascinating name that seems to suggest a hill that shoots up and down. Little is left of its woodlands except in private parks and gardens; but trees are still a feature of the Oxfordshire countryside, not least on the beautiful slopes bordering the upper reaches of the Thames. In the south-east of the county the Chilterns retain the character that much of the county once bore, while in the north-east the Forest of Bernwood overspreads the Buckinghamshire border near Bicester, where the first element in the name of both the forest and the town is the Old English *byrgen*, 'burial mound'.

Although dwindled now, these south Midland forests retained their character unmodified to any great extent until Norman times, when their potentialities for sport brought them under the protection of the Forest Laws. Henry I built a hunting-lodge at Woodstock and enclosed a park there. Consequently we find the district dotted with such place-names as Kingstanding Farm in Wychwood parish, Buckleap Copse and Sore Leap, in which 'sore' is the term for a buck in its fourth year.

Warwickshire, in contrast, lacks royal forests. This may surprise Shakespearians to whom Arden, the scene of so much of *As You Like It*, is the forest above all other forests. The question turns on definition. In Law, a forest was a region subject to the Forest Acts, which Arden escaped; but it was nevertheless a vast extent of woodland north of the Avon which had the effect of separating Warwickshire north of the river from Warwickshire south of it. The Hwicce had entered the territory from the Avon after sailing up the Severn, and had occupied much of the south-east of the present county, including Roman Alcester, before the eighth century. The most significant name in the extreme south is Tysoe. There are three of them: Upper, Middle and Lower, and they are held by experts to provide the first really unequivocal evidence for the worship of the god Tiw, whose name survives in Tuesday. The name means 'spur of land dedicated to Tiw', and refers to the branch of the main ridge of the Cotswolds which forms the south-eastern boundary of the Vale of the Red Horse, a name which in turn commemorates the figure of a horse, presumably cut in honour of the war-god, to celebrate a victory won by the Anglo-Saxons. Such a cutting clearly shows that the Hwicce had reached the district while the worship of Tiw was still in full vigour. Between Banbury and Bicester is Souldern, where a pagan Saxon cemetery of pre-AD 500 has been discovered. Two miles away is Tusmore, 'a lake haunted by a giant demon'. 'Tus' may be the name of a heathen God, which would be further confirmation of early settlement, and there are other isolated reminders of heathenism in the South Midlands, particularly in the Anglian region between the Middle Nene and the Ouse.

Celtic names are rare in the region: but Brailes Hill, with Upper and Lower Brailes taking their names from it in the way so many Saxon settlements took their names from hills, seems to contain the Welsh *bre* (hill) in the first part, with at least the possibility of the second part being derived from *les*, the 'court, palace or residence of a chieftain'. Mancetter (Manduessedun) is Romano-British, and Cosford may be Cossa's ford, but equally it may be derived from an earlier name of the river Swift. Many names in this part of Warwickshire incorporate -ing, but usually with -ton added, which makes them later than the -ings derived from *ingas*.

In the north of the county the scene is completely transformed by such large industrial centres as Birmingham and Coventry, which sprawl across infertile country on the border of Staffordshire, where the great forests of Kinver, Morfe, and Cannock Chase, which were royal forests and therefore subject to the Forest Laws, affected development. Consequently the villages in the north are smaller than might be expected, having regard to the size of the total population of the area. The reason for this is the same as elsewhere in such districts: namely, that small hamlets could only be established piecemeal as the trees were felled, and as the land was of low fertility, progress was slow. So early names are rare. It has been suggested that Willey means 'temple or holy place', from the Old English *weoh*. It is more likely to mean 'willow wood', and Wolvey probably simply means an enclosure to protect flocks from wolves.

On a hill in the sparsely populated district of Long Compton stand the Rollright Stones, the county's only megalithic monument, and only one of these, the 'King's Stone', is in Warwickshire. Among the few other ancient monuments in Warwickshire are the village forts at Beausale and Claverdon, and the chieftain's dwelling at Brinklow. Wappenbury, between Leamington and Rugby, has a name that can hardly fail to catch the eye. It is only a small village now, but must have been important at one time. The visitor will be curious about a ramparted enclosure and a green road leading to a crossing of the Leam.

Ancient roads provide the frame, in the literal sense, in which urban Warwickshire grew. The Fosse Way, Watling Street and the Icknield Way practically enclosed it, and the Icknield Way, which cut through the forest on the west in skirting the Cotswolds, opened up the district now associated with the city of Birmingham, which takes its name from a people of whom we know virtually nothing. There were probably Roman settlements in the region, but they would not be of much consequence except at Alcester, probably built to guard the road as it passed through the forest, and the towns with 'Street' as part of their names, of which Stratford-on-Avon is the most important. Others are Stretton Baskerville, near Watling Street; Street Ashton, near the Fosse; Stretton-on-the-Fosse; Stretton-under-Fosse, and Stretton on Dunsmore.

The castles at Warwick and Kenilworth have always been scenes of romance and tragedy. Scott's *Kenilworth* makes one an evocative name, Warwick owes much to its incomparable setting. It takes its name from the Saxon *Wearingas*, who settled the western plain of the county. The castle itself is the successor of the stronghold built by Ethelfleda, Lady of the Mercians, the daughter of Alfred the Great. The town was a royal borough at Domesday. These powerful martial centres eventually had the monastic foundations to reckon with. Coventry had a convent founded about 650 by St Osburg and refounded in 1043 by Leofric, Earl of Mercia; Nuneaton takes its name from a nunnery refounded before 1155. These refoundings are significant because the main effects of the Norman Conquest in Warwickshire and the neighbouring counties were the result of the reconstitution of the ecclesiastical control of the region. Lichfield had been the most important diocese in the Mercian kingdom, extending as far north as the Ribble. In 1124 the abbey of Coventry was paired with Lichfield and made the twin ecclesiastical centre of the Midlands. The Coventry pageants show how influential the Church was in the Middle Ages here as elsewhere.

1 Lambourn, Berkshire: 'stream where lambs are washed'

2 Corfe Castle, Dorset: 'the castle of the pass, or cutting'
3 Ludlow, Shropshire: 'hill by the rapid'

4 Cheddar Gorge, Somerset: from an Old English word meaning pouch, here used for cave

5 Clovelly, Devon: the most likely source is the Celtic *clawdd*, 'trench'

6 Brown Willy, Cornwall: a corruption of *Bryn Huel*, 'the tin mine ridge'

7 The Malvern Hills, Worcestershire: from the Welsh *moel*, 'bare'; *bryn*, 'hill'

8 Chittlehampton, Devon: the home of the people of the *cietel*, 'the valley among hills'

9 Minchinhampton, Gloucestershire: 'the nuns' hampton', signifying its ownership by the nunnery at Caen

10 Lower Slaughter, Gloucestershire: 'slough or muddy place', unique among English place-names in using the word

11 Much Wenlock, Shropshire: 'white church or monastery', from the Welsh *gwyn-loc*

12 Wendover, Buckinghamshire: 'white river', from *gwyn-dwfr*, referring to the chalk stream

13 Cartmel, Lancashire: 'sandbank by rocky ground', from the Old Norse *kart-melr*

14 Coniston Water: 'the king's manor', from *Coningeston*

15 Watendlath, Lake District: 'the hill at the end of the lake'; from *vatn*, 'lake'; *hlaw*, 'hill'; with *endi*, 'end', contracted between
16 Penzance, Cornwall: 'the holy headland', *pen-sans*

17 Muker in Swaledale, Yorkshire: 'the narrow field in the dale of the swilling stream', from the Old Norse *miór*, 'narrow'; *akr*, 'field'; swillan, 'to wash'

18 Penyghent, Yorkshire: 'the hill of the open country', *pen y gaint*
19 Roche, Cornwall: from the French *roche*, 'rock'. The ruined
chapel is evidence of 13th century colonisation of the moorland

20 Blanchland, Northumberland: 'white land'. A surprising name until we find that it was derived from Blanche-lande, Normandy

21 Durham: from *Dunholm*, 'hill on an island'. The present form of the name is due to Norman influence

Rugby, which first appears as Rocheberie, perhaps meaning 'burh of the rocks', is to be noted as having the Scandinavian *by* as its terminal, and Scandinavian names are rare in Warwickshire. Among the few instances are Monks Kirby, and Wibtoft, near High Cross, where the Fosse Way crosses Watling Street. There is a curious Warwickshire superstition that the dwarf elder only grew where the blood of a Dane had been spilt. Another curious custom that may be associated with the Danes is the collecting of wroth silver at Ryton-on-Dunsmore by the agent of the Duke of Buccleuch, lord of the manor of the Hundred of Knightlow. The ritual took place on Knightlow Hill at sunrise – suggesting sun worship – on Martinmas Day. The penalty for non-payment was a white bull with red nose and ears. The topographical significance of the custom is that the point at which the money was paid, the stump of an ancient cross on a tumulus with four fir trees said to represent four knights killed and buried there, is near the Danish border, and the Danes produced legends to sustain their rule as the Romans produced roads.

The boundary between Danish Northamptonshire and Anglian Warwickshire was Watling Street. It marked the limit of Scandinavian settlement in the south Midlands and explains the infrequency of Scandinavian names in Warwickshire. The boundary line now accepted has been questioned occasionally by those who have pointed out that there are few Scandinavian village names between Kettering and Market Harborough; but if early forms are examined it will be seen that this is not so. Eckland means 'oak grove' and Loatland 'grove with hollows'. Copeland is from the Old Norse for 'bought land'. Hesland is from *Lesli lundr*, which means 'hazel grove'. The point to note in these names is that they illustrate how, when the Scandinavians displaced the Old English in place-names, the substituted name tended to be descriptive. Here they also show that this part of the county was woodland at the time of the Danish settlement.

The main clues to the early settlement of Northamptonshire are to be found in the place-names along the valleys of the Nene and its tributaries. Oundle, Thrapston, Irthlingborough, Billing and Kettering are all old, and incidentally the river Ise at Kettering is a derivation of Ouse. But even these names do not go back to the earliest river-bank settlements. The Romano-British had come up the rivers, and settlements were already established along the Nene, and in the region between Northampton and Daventry in the north and Towcester in the south in Roman times.

A break in the line of old place-names is clearly to be seen in the middle of the Nene valley, which is obviously attributable to the density of the woodland in this part of the Forest of Rockingham. Only one old name occurs, that of Benefield, 'the feld of *Bera's* people', which despite its apparently later form is undoubtedly of great antiquity. When the forest is crossed and the Welland valley reached, old names again occur in Cottingham and Rockingham; but the only ancient place-name between the middle Nene and the Ouse is Gidding in western Huntingdonshire. The explanation of this appears to be that there was continuous woodland between Rushden (rushy dene) and Whittlewood, which would form a barrier between the fertile plain of eastern Northamptonshire and that of western Bedfordshire, where Melchbourne suggests fertile pastures where the cows gave a rich supply of milk, as no doubt they still do. The Anglian settlement of the Nene Valley must have been in considerable force. The three names, Wellingborough, Orlingbury and Kislingbury, can hardly be later than the sixth century.

The Eastern Midlands, as we shall see presently, had been divided up among the Danish armies early in the tenth century, and each had been given its own administrative centre, which under the Normans became county towns. Northampton was well placed for another. It was probably already settled, and certainly had established villages all round it. So the Danes made Northampton to the south Midlands what Southampton was to the south of England, and the two were connected by the road that ran through Brackley, Oxford, Abingdon, Newbury, Whitchurch and Winchester. The effect of the Scandinavian occupation of Northamptonshire is seen in the number of -thorpe and -by terminals in the county. There are five Ashbys, showing that woodland was still a feature, and indeed woodland terms are frequent in the county. There are at least thirteen other names ending in -by. But the number of Scandinavian names is still nothing like so great as in some other counties, and there remained a strong distinction racially and socially between the Danish settlements in the north and the Anglo-Saxon settlements in the south, which continued to have closer affinities with Bedfordshire and Buckinghamshire. This is shown in the number of names ending in -cot, of which there are more than thirty examples in the county, twelve within four or five miles of Towcester, and twenty-three near the western border of the county. These cots or cotes suggest humble settlements.

The other four counties in the South Midlands, Bedfordshire, Buckinghamshire, Huntingdonshire and Hertfordshire, all lack historical entity when studied from the place-name point of view. Their geographical situation and consequential ease of access led to racial complexities that are not readily sorted out. It seems reasonably clear that the settlement of Bedfordshire was earlier than that of Buckinghamshire; but if there was settlement at a very early date by invaders it has left singularly little trace in the place-names on the map to-day. There is little evidence in support of settlement before 571, although the large burial mound at Kempston, situated at a sharp bend of the Ouse, yielded objects proving conclusively that Saxons and Angles had produced a combined culture in the Ouse valley before the end of the sixth century. The names Pillinge, near Wootton, and Kitchen, near Pulloxhill, may also be late sixth-century.

Huntingdonshire would be the first of the four to be settled, apart from the settlement from the Thames in Buckinghamshire. Yet only a small part of Huntingdonshire can have been attractive to the Saxons, which makes it remarkable that the county has such early names as Gidding, Yelling and Wintringham. The last named is found also in the Yorkshire Wolds and in Lincolnshire at points where the earliest Anglian invaders established themselves. Another early name is Earith on the edge of the Fens. The same name is found at Erith in Kent in a region that is believed to have been settled in the fifth century. Celtic names are extremely rare in Bedfordshire and Huntingdonshire. Three names, however, in Bedfordshire show settlement before the middle of the seventh century. They are the Harrowdens, Weedon Beck and Weedon Lois, all obviously centres of heathen worship. There is another Harrowden (*hearh*, meaning Idol or temple) in Northamptonshire.

If we try to follow the lines suggested by the available evidence we reach the conclusion that the Saxons who came in from the south-west met the Angles who came in from the north-east and settled together in Bedfordshire and Huntingdonshire, and that the process was in the nature of an infiltration that continued over a lengthy period. This integration is believed on high authority to explain the large number of names ending in hoe, 'hill, spur'. This is so distinctive a feature of the place-names of Bedfordshire and Huntingdonshire that the authorities argue that it could only have been the result of a unique racial group developing its own system of local nomenclature. Several of these would come into use during the Danish wars, particularly where *tôt*, 'look-out hill' is incorporated, as in Totternhoe, which also contains *aerne*, meaning 'house'. The name therefore means 'a dwelling for the watch'.

Ward's Hurst, Pitstone in Buckinghamshire means 'wooded hill from which watch was kept'.

If Huntingdonshire lacks a substantial number of names that assist historical dating, apart from the Danish pocket in the Hundreds of Norman Cross and Toseland, it is rich in names that stir the imagination and provoke speculation. One such is Coppingford, which means 'the ford of the traders'. The ford in question lies west of the village. It has a cart track on one side and a footpath on the other. It may be that the track was the ancient Bullock Road that branched off Ermine Street southwest of Coppingford. Ermine Street here was distinctively a British trackway. It ran from Caesar's Camp in Bedfordshire by way of Toseland, and continued through Weston and Upton to enter Northamptonshire at Wansford. The Roman road of that name followed the same course, but entered Huntingdonshire from Cambridgeshire near Papworth St Agnes, to follow the old course through Godmanchester, where two important roads intersect. The *Via Devana* approached Godmanchester from Fenny Stanton and continued to Clapton in Northamptonshire. It was along these roads that the Danes travelled to destroy the great abbeys at Peterborough, Crowland and Ely.

From this destructive progress the subsequent history of the place-names in the region is to be read, and it is coloured by the Danish habit of introducing romantic stories to account for what happened. Even to this day men of Scandinavian descent seldom spoil a good story in the telling for want of inventive fertility! Thus we are told that in 967 the abbey of Ramsey was built on the island where a solitary ram, 'armed by Nature's cunning with twisted and crooked horns, took up his abode and left his lasting name to the place.' In the same vein we are told that St Ives was the name given to the Saxon town of Slepe after a ploughman had turned up the remains of the body of a man revealed in a vision to be none other than St Ive, a Persian archbishop who had conducted a mission in England. Another town in Huntingdonshire changed its name to St Neots, after a Cornish saint had been conveyed to a place called Ainulphsbury, where a monastery was founded in his honour. Nor were these legends confined to saints. King's Delph Gate in Farcet has the Old English word for a trench, pit or quarry, still found in the North of England for quarry. The story here is that either Canute or his queen, fearing the boisterousness of the waves on Whittlesey Mere, caused a ditch to be dug.

So if many place-names in Huntingdonshire are problematical in their

origin, no-one need be at a loss for a plausible source, and when we come
to the name of the county town, with a choice between '*Hunta's* hill' and
'the huntsman's hill', it would be completely out of character to plump
for anyone but the huntsman.

It seems remarkable that in both Bedfordshire and Huntingdonshire
so many names can only be traced through records back to the thirteenth
century, even where monasteries were established in their towns. Of the
two, Bedfordshire has the better documentation, particularly in relation
to Luton and the Romano-British settlements at Dunstable, Bedford and
Sandy. It is now a county in which research is active and results may be
expected.

Buckinghamshire as an independent entity does not appear in records
until 1016. Its earlier history can best be traced in place-names that fall
into two distinct groups, those north of the Chilterns and those south of
them. It has no monasteries or castles with legends attached, and its
most renowned ancient monument, the great mound at Taplow, cov-
ering the body and grave furniture of the Saxon noble who gave the place
its name, belongs to the Thames Valley settlement. North of the Chilterns a British population has left its record in such names as Brill (containing the Welsh *bre*), an ancient settlement where Edward the Confessor had a palace; Chetwode (containing the Celtic *Kaito*, allied to the
Welsh *coed*); Brickhill (containing the Welsh *brig* 'top, mound') and
others. Coming down to Saxon times we find Wing, Oving, Halling and
the obscure but certainly archaic name, Kimble, as well as early personal names incorporated in the Missendens and Mentmore, all indicating earlier settlement than anything to be found in Bedfordshire.
Wendover in the same area is derived from the original British name,
meaning 'white stream', and corresponding with the Welsh *gwyn dwfr*,
'white river', a name descriptive of the chalk in the bed of the local
stream. Kimble Castle is south of Wendover, near Ellesborough (Esla's
hill), where Cunobelinus of Colchester – Shakespeare's Cymbeline –
won a victory, according to tradition; but experts believe that the battle
was fought near Buckingham, leaving Ellesborough to lick its sores with
the less romantic distinction of having a Gallows Hill.

Buckinghamshire is the land of Bucca's people. It has neither the *boc*
'beech' of Buckham in Hampshire and Buckhurst Hill in Essex, nor the
male deer of Buckfast in Devon and Buckden in Yorkshire. Nor again is it
related to the many Bucklands that meant land held by book, or charter.
The choice of Buckingham as the county town was strategic. The com-

petition was between its peninsula site and the situation of Aylesbury on Akeman Street, which ran from Tring through Aylesbury to Bicester. Another apparently descriptive name in Buckinghamshire is Chesham Bois, in which 'Bois' is in fact derived less romantically from the De Bosco or De Bois family and is therefore manorial.

The Buckinghamshire volume of the English Place-Name Society has other examples of contributions to regal and baronial social history found in the county's place-names, which might be thought appropriate for one that continues to be something of a national shop-window through the presence of the Prime Minister's country house at Chequers. Quainton (the queen's manor), for example, shows that before the Norman Conquest women could own land and give their names to their manors. The Risboroughs, Monks and Princes, are so named because one belonged to the Church, the other to the Crown. Monks Risborough belonged to Christ Church, Canterbury, Princes Risborough to the Black Prince, who acquired the manor in 1343. It had formerly been a royal manor; but in 1337 it was in the possession of the Earl of Cornwall and was known as Earls Risborough. Another Buckinghamshire place-name with regal overtones is Farnham Royal, in which the first part is 'fernham', the second part arose from the manor being held by the grand serjeanty of supporting the king's arm at his Coronation. The village's proximity to Windsor and the noble pleasance of Burnham Beeches enables it to retain its royal name with dignity.

Norman associations with the county are rarer than we might expect. We have them in the place-names of Newport Pagnell, Stoke Mandeville and Weston Turville, where the remains of the motte and bailey of the castle are still to be seen; but few of the great French families appear to have been influential in Buckinghamshire, which remained sparsely populated in the north until the Middle Ages. The Chilterns separated north from south more effectively than similar ranges elsewhere. The explanation of this is that unlike the South Downs, for example, the Chilterns were great masses of chalk unbroken by water gaps. So lines of communication could only be through what were called wind gaps. The most notable of these is the one that was used for the road that passed through from High Wycombe, which contains the Old English combe for valley, to Princes Risborough, Tring and Aylesbury. Another gap is found at the head of the Ver valley. It would probably be wrong to think of the Chilterns being uninhabited before the Norman Conquest. There were at least two ancient trackways over them, and it seems reasonable to suppose that small settlements would be established at favourable points along these. What is, however, indisputable is that the British would hold out longer against invaders there than elsewhere, as they did in other hill country we have passed through in earlier chapters.

In Hertfordshire the contrast between one part of the county and another is less between north and south, as in Buckinghamshire, than between east and west; but it is very marked. Hertfordshire lacks basic unity. Nowhere do its rivers or streams form boundaries strong enough to separate one region from another; but in a variety of ways it is a 'betwixt and between' region. The north has strong affinities with Huntingdonshire, particularly near Royston, where the Roman Ermine Street and the pre-Roman Icknield Way cross each other and link the town with East Anglia and the Midlands to the north and west. The east of Hertfordshire long formed part of the kingdom of the East Saxons and was in the old diocese of London. The capital and the whole of Middlesex had become part of the East Saxon kingdom by the 6th century and early in the 8th the kings of Essex were still able to issue charters in respect of land in Middlesex. Most of this is now included in the deanery of Braughing, a name that suggests occupation of the region before rather than after the middle of the sixth century, while Tewin, 'the people of Tiwa', again takes us back to the days of heathen worship.

The clue to the early settlement of the east of the county is clearly related to that of Essex and would develop from the Thames by way of the Lea valley, whereas the early settlement in the north would be from well drained ridgeways. Elsewhere, Hertfordshire long remained a deeply wooded county into which Anglo-Saxon infiltration was inevitably slow and laborious, with the result that the place-names of the centre and the west tend to be of single homesteads, or small hamlets, settled by the persistent folk who felled the trees and brought the gravel terraces along the river banks into cultivation. When King Edgar gave Hatfield to the monastery of Ely he did so 'because, since the county is wooded, the brethren can find timber for the fabric of their church, and wood sufficient for their other purposes.'

It was suggested by Sir Mortimer Wheeler that for many years after the first Saxon invasions London, which was still in British hands, had defences sufficiently strong to prevent the penetration of English settlers from the north-west into the woodlands of Middlesex and Hertfordshire, and that the 'Grim's Ditches' of Hertfordshire, Middlesex and Buckinghamshire were raised by the English who had settled in the southern

Midlands to prevent the still independent Britons to the south moving north to expel them. The frequent use of the element 'bury' in the Home Counties is puzzling. Many of these are moated. The history of the dwellings so named does not go back beyond the Middle Ages, but they may succeed earlier defended sites. In view of Sir Mortimer Wheeler's opinion it may be significant that in the northern parish of Reed, the highest in Hertfordshire, there are six 'burys', and the church has late Anglo-Saxon work in the nave.

The evidence of late occupation of Hertfordshire by the Anglo-Saxons found in the place-names is confirmed by archaeology. Nothing has been found in the county to support early settlement, although at Luton in Bedfordshire, only four miles over the border, Anglo-Saxon settlement appears to have begun by the beginning of the fifth century. Drawing these several threads together we reach the general conclusion that the Anglo-Saxons entered mid-Hertfordshire from the north-east to establish themselves on the chalk around Hitchin, which is derived from an ancient tribal name found also in Bedfordshire, while British names survive in Walsworth, Walden, as well as in the survivals of heathen cultures at Wain Wood and Thundridge.

These various factors have contributed to Hertfordshire's retention of a rural landscape, with several small towns and villages that to many people continue to typify the England that built up our most characteristic way of life. The county town itself had only fourteen thousand inhabitants in 1951. St Albans, which is to Hertfordshire what Colchester is to Essex, is still a country town no less than an ecclesiastical city. As Verulamium it was one of the most important Roman towns in Britain. The Saxon Abbey, built on an eminence above Verulamium, was one of the greatest. In 1154 its head was made premier abbot of England. Watling Street passes through the city. In fact one of its earlier names is that of the tribe that gave its name to the street. Yet despite all the factors that might have gone to submerge it beneath industrial development, St Albans retains its unique character, and nowhere is this felt more than as one makes one's way up the winding trail of Fishpool Street, first trodden by the pilgrims who by-passed Verulamium to reach the shrine of the martyred saint.

CHAPTER SIX
Essex and East Anglia

ESSEX · SUFFOLK · NORFOLK
CAMBRIDGESHIRE AND THE ISLE OF ELY

Essex and East Anglia grew up as it were, back to back, not side by side – the one from the Thames, the other from the Wash. In the settlement made between Alfred the Great and the Danes, Essex was placed under the Danelaw; but in the event of the Danes interfered little with its Saxon way of life. Only in the Walton-on-the-Naze district do we get in the Sokens a pocket of place-names that are indisputably Scandinavian. Even Clacton, which used to be thought akin, is now held to be Old English.

The East Saxon kingdom makes its first appearance under Ethelbert of Kent at the end of the 6th century. Its king, Sebert, had married Ethelbert's sister and acknowledged his brother-in-law as overlord, although much of Kent was Jutish while Essex was Saxon. Then in 604 the East Saxons received the Christian faith from Mellitus, bishop of London, which at that time was included in Essex, and it was largely as the result of this ecclesiastical influence that the East Saxon kingdom spread westward to take in eastern Hertfordshire, with the effect on its place-names already referred to.

Since the Saxons came into what became Essex from the Thames and its tributaries, this early link with the country to the south and west, rather than with that to the north, is what might have been expected; but we might still be surprised to find how far they penetrated. The most impressive proof of this is the rich burial mound at Broomfield, which contained furnishings comparable with those at Taplow. Among the many -ingas place-names in Essex, six occur in the upper reaches of the Lea and its tributary the Stort. In fact, -ingas place names in Essex are only less numerous than those in Sussex. Epping was the place where the men of the upland lived, Nazeing was the home of the people who lived on the naze or ness.

The early place-names in mid- and south-Essex are closely akin to those of both Sussex and Kent. In some cases they are identical counterparts. Feering corresponds with Ferring, Barling with the Birlings of both Sussex and Kent. Patching, near Broomfield, and Tillingham are both matched in Sussex, and Bobbing and Halling in Kent have the same personal name origins as Bobbingworth and the Hallingburys in Essex. Even more conclusive of the relationship are the names ending in -ge for district. Vange, 'the district of the fen folk', was formerly more extensive than it is now; but the most important example was *Ginges*, a district south-west of Chelmsford, which included the modern parishes of Ingatestone, Fryerning, Margaretting, Mountnessing, Buttesbury, Stock, Ingrave and at least part of East Horndon. So large an administrative district could only indicate sparsity of population, since in Sussex two or three -ingas may be included in a single modern parish. The names Ingatestone, Margaretting, and Ingrave take their names from the *Gigingas*.

Several instances of heathen place-names have been mentioned in connection with places dedicated to the worship of Thunor or Woden in other counties. There are in fact more of them in Essex than in any other Saxon region. There are also names that are evidence of local belief in demons, or goblins, and water sprites. Examples are Shackmore in Lawford and Nickerlands in Stanford Rivers. All show that despite the mission of Mellitus, which was followed by that of Cedd fifty years later, heathen beliefs were strong and flourishing in Essex when the Saxons gave these places their names. Even as late as Shakespeare's time, superstitious beliefs remained so strong that Archbishop Harsnett, an Essex man, while vicar of Chigwell inveighed against 'certain egregious popish impostures', which he associated with demonology, and some of the names of demons mentioned by him are used by Edgar in *King Lear*.

The paucity of archaeological finds in Essex has led some authorities to see it as proof of the poverty and backwardness of the kingdom. It is also true that in no other part of England are there so few pre-Roman or even pre-Saxon names. But surely the former is due to the intensity with which the land has been worked for so many centuries, obliterating earthworks that might have stood out if more of the area had remained as moorland or heath. And the latter is due to the completeness of the Saxon colonisation of the county. As for poverty, it must be remembered that Caesar was able to feed his legions off the land, and in a short time had a surplus of grain for export. Nevertheless the size of the ancient parishes does support the view that the population was small when they were formed, and the county may well have been poor in the south-west corner and the more heavily wooded areas, especially where water was in short supply.

There were early settlements along the bank of the Thames at Fobbing, Mucking, and Corringham, and on hill-top sites like Horndon-on-the-Hill, which were above flood level, so the people who lived in them could turn out their cattle on the marshes and have secure land to which they could retreat. They may be compared with the Polden villages in Somerset. All along this line of early settlements we find the 'wicks' that indicate dairy farms at which cheeses were made.

The rich land to the east was also settled early, resulting in such place-names as Wakering, Fingringhoe, and Dengie, a name derived from the *Daengingas*, and when we reach the north-east tip of the county we have the land that had been cleared for the Saxons by the Romano-British round Colchester.

In the Tendring Hundred the most marked feature is the large number of villages with names ending in -ley. In the extreme north-east we have Ardleigh, Little Bromley, Mistley, Little Bentley, Great Bromley, Great Bentley and Weeley – the ley with a heathen temple. These are derived from the Old English *leah*, 'a clearing', indicating that this was a heavily wooded region cleared by men from the earlier settlements at Frinton, Walton and Clacton. In fact, Tendring may orginally have been the name of the whole peninsula, and be connected etymologically with Thanet in Kent. There is another crop of -ley endings in the Rochford Hundred in Hockley, Rayleigh, Hadleigh, Leigh which are all contiguous and reach their eastern extremity in Eastwood, which suggests that it was so-named because it was the limit of the woodland cleared in this drive. To the east of it, Canewdon and Ashingdon are names of hills, Prittlewell and Hawkwell names of springs, and the indication in their names of early bridges at Stambridge and Fambridge might suggest that the Rochford Hundred was fully settled both early and in strength; but the number of villages bearing the name 'bridge', when compared with the number of large towns with 'ford' as their suffix, has puzzled many. The explanation must be that the introduction of 'bridge' came late. Bridge towns of importance, with a Saxon element in them, are extremely rare. Brixton and Bristol are two. The 'bridge' in Cambridge came late. In its earlier form it may have contained the Celtic *rhyd*, a ford. To this may be added the evidence that the settlements now engulfed in Southend-on-Sea all point to the whole of this fertile country, with rich black soil comparable with that of Holland, being prosperous when much of the country inland languished. In Leigh it had a port and point of entry that much of the coast to the west lacked.

The first Saxon villages were established between half a mile and a mile from the river bank, according to the danger of flooding, leaving rich loam terraces free for crops. They were circular in form, and built round an open space which may survive as a village green. We can still identify many of these and find in them confirmation of age. If its name did not betray it we should still suspect from the size of its green that Hatfield Heath in west Essex was not one of these first settlements. It obviously belongs to a time of greater security. Inland from the riverside villages the land would be cleared for pasture, a process greatly assisted by the oxen, always greedy feeders as well as being heavy beasts that trampled the ground in their eagerness to get at the saplings and seedlings. In this way, the line of the woodland was constantly in process of being pushed back, eventually producing the long narrow strips that survive as the elongated parishes of the Thames Estuary, counterparts of those in East Sussex mentioned earlier.

In course of time it came about that the animals were being fed too far away for convenience and a new settlement was founded. It was in this way that the map of Essex came to be dotted over with 'ends' and 'tyes'. They already covered the face of the county at Domesday, and the point about them is that they indicate family rather than communal settlement, and are in contrast to the villages of Cambridgeshire, which are nucleated, with large fields for cultivation outside. In some Essex parishes the settlement is so scattered that there is hardly a centre of any kind, even round the church. The parish with the largest number of these tiny hamlets is Great Waltham, which has ten 'ends' and four 'streets'. Writtle on the other side of Chelmsford was another large forest parish, and so was Waltham Abbey on the Lea. The other large groups that may be compared with the *inges* are the Rodings and the Colnes, which must have developed from the Roman roads that ran near them, but which got their present names from Normans. South of the Rodings were the *Haeferingas* whose territory extended to the Thames at Dagenham. Their name survives in Havering.

All the old towns of Essex are strung along the great Roman roads linking London with Colchester and Colchester with St Albans, forming the triangle on which the whole superstructure of this part of Roman England was constructed. Those in the north marked the extremity of Saxon infiltration at the time they were constructed; those in the south are at fords: Ilford, Romford, Stratford, Woodford, Chelmsford, and so forth. Despite this, few Roman names remain. As Isaac Taylor, who was descended from the Taylors of Ongar and Stanford Rivers, said: 'The Saxon civilisation was domestic, the genius of Rome was imperial; the Saxons colonised, the Romans conquered. Hence the traces of Roman rule which remain upon the map are surprisingly few in number'. It is this Saxon character that still makes Essex so homely and so lovable.

The other area of early settlement was the north-west, where we find the villages of the chalk downland around Saffron Walden: Manuden, Clavering, Arkesden, Elmdon, Littlebury and the Chesterfords, all of great charm and comparable with the villages of the Braughing deanery of Hertfordshire. Of these, Chesterford and Littlebury are names that indicate early encampment. Littlebury and Spellbrook in Little Hallingbury have Iron Age camps near them, and both contain elements meaning 'speech hill'. Related to these are Mutlow, meaning 'moot hill', in Wendens Ambo (which means both Wendens), the meeting place of the Uttlesford Hundred, and Toot Hill in Stanford Rivers, which was the meeting place of the Ongar Hundred, while Harlow, the adjoining Hundred, may have meant 'temple mound'. Other defended settlements of which traces remain in earthworks are found across the whole of the county, but notably at Pleshey, Danbury and Castle Hedingham.

That the middle portion of the northern band across Essex was settled much later is shown in the descriptive terminals of the place-names. East of Thaxted, between the Stour and the Roman Stane Street running through Dunmow we have the -fields: the Bardfields, Finchingfield, Wethersfield, Gosfield and the rest of them, and alongside them the -steads: Maplestead, Twinstead, Halstead, Greenstead; but with a few -hams: the Yeldhams and Hedinghams, along the old road into Suffolk.

Running over the county in this rather cursory but curiously revealing manner we reach the conclusion that the place-names of north- and mid-Essex indicate later colonisation than those of Kent to the south or East Anglia to the north. History supports that conclusion, and topography supplies much of the answer. Apart from the cliffs at Leigh-on-Sea and Prittlewell, the heath around Colchester and the downland in the north-west, forest and marsh rendered most of the county inaccessible except from the rivers. The clearing of the forest and the draining of the marshes was a slow process; but when it was accomplished Essex and East Anglia came into the close association that has led so many writers to treat Essex as though it were part of East Anglia, which it is not and never was, although in the upper reaches of the Stour (the historical boundary between the two) there have been curious gains and losses in recent times. And nearer the mouth of the Stour the villages on both sides of the river have come to be called the Constable Country. Anyone not familiar with the district would be at a loss to distinguish between the places on the Essex bank and those on the Suffolk bank as they appear in the paintings. Even the place-names establish relationship. There are two Bergholts, the one in which Constable was born on the Suffolk bank, West Bergholt on the Essex bank, and both mean 'copse by a hill' – possibly 'birch copse'. There is also Bures on both banks. Having regard to the long separation of these two regions, the similarities and duplications bear out Sir Frank Stenton's opinion* 'that the study of English place-names has not yet established any fundamental distinctions between the local nomenclature of Anglian, Saxon, and Jutish territory'. He continued: 'As evidence for the Continental origins of the English people the differences between the heathen cultures of Anglian and Saxon England, though real, are less significant than the resemblances'.

These resemblances continued until later times. A tract of open country cleared of woodland is a 'field' in Suffolk as it is in Essex and Sussex. It is less likely to be found so called in the West Country, although there is some evidence for the view that the use of 'field' for a fenced-in piece of ground only came in after the Black Death in the middle of the fourteenth century, by which time most places had acquired names. Despite these similarities, however, the name Saxham, found in Suffolk, and Saxton in Cambridgeshire, suggest that these Saxon settlements were regarded as alien elements. There are several other pockets of aliens in East Anglia, which is not surprising having regard to the proximity of the Continent. So in Swaffham, found in Norfolk and Cambridgeshire, we have evidence of one of the earliest settlers, the Swabians who, like the Frisians of Friston in Suffolk came from the same district as the Saxons in their homeland. A less obvious link with the Frisians is Hengrave, in which the 'grave' was *gred*, the Frisian word for pasture. Whissonsett and Witchingham on the Wensum commemorate the Wicingas, who made a piratical attack on East Anglia in 841. Flempton in Suffolk is the -ton of the Flemings.

Anglo-Saxon England, p. 7.

There are so many of these folk names in East Anglia that it must be accepted that the East Angles were a federation of smaller peoples who integrated into a single group in what has always been an isolated part of England. Those who know it well would even go so far as to say that there are times when the separateness of East Anglia in the far east is as strong as that of Cornwall in the far west, despite the fact that on one signpost may be seen directions to New York and California. We have seen how East Anglia was cut off from Essex. It was just as much cut off from Middle Anglia by the Fens. We know that the Roman roads linking Colchester with Norwich and Cambridge fell into disuse, which meant that the only way open to those who wanted to travel west – and they would have asked, why should they? – was along the ancient trackway that was already two thousand years old when the Saxons arrived: the Icknield Way. The massive earthworks to be found along its course – practically all post-Roman – show how determined the tribes on either side were to preserve their independence. It is probable that the villages on the Cambridgeshire uplands with 'West' as part of their name, for which there are no counterparts with 'East' as their forename, mark the western extremity of colonisation in East Anglia, suggesting that the Cam in Cambridge was the boundary between East Anglia and Mercia.

So for our purpose East Anglia is the kingdom founded in 575 by Uffa, whose name lives on in Ufford, and is made up of Suffolk, the land of the south folk, Norfolk, the land of the north folk, Cambridgeshire and the Isle of Ely, a region which in the ninth century was invaded by the Vikings and remained a Danish kingdom until conquered by Edward the Elder in 921. Entry to this large area had always been principally from the Wash, which had drawn invaders like a magnet. What puzzled scholars in the past was that these invaders should have thought it worth their while to press on when they discovered what a desolate and waterlogged country they had entered. It long appeared to topographers that the only firm land was in the patches of rising ground on which Ely, Crowland and March stand. In recent years air photography, followed by excavation, has established that many places that later became waterlogged were formerly inhabited and cultivated. Places near the Icknield Way, from which Ickleton takes its name, support the view. Dykes constructed by the Iceni, earthworks at Castle Hill, Cambridge, round moats at Fowlmere and pit dwellings at Barrington all bear testimony to early occupation.

The Roman army expanded the existing system of roadways, making great use of the Icknield Way. Ermine Street was constructed to cross the region from Godmanchester to Royston, leaving its name in Arrington and Armingford. Akeman Street ran through Ely, where Etheldred founded a monastery which was followed by others at Thornley in Cambridgeshire, Peterborough (with a name that is a whole history in itself), Ramsey and Crowland. All these are clues to later settlements; but of early Anglo-Saxon settlements it is disappointing to find not a single -ingas place-name in the whole of Cambridgeshire, and despite the inroads of the Danes not a single ancient -by or -thorp. So for our knowledge of the progress of occupation we have to concentrate on the roads and the watercourses. A section of the Icknield Way is called 'cattle road', reminding us of the centuries-old use of the marshes for fattening cattle; Oldemere in Whittlesey tells us that this was the site of a vanished lake. The Dittons are the -tons of the ditches. The raised banks of flood plains are called 'noddons'. When we examine the river system we find striking evidence of the way so many of them have changed their courses. The most remarkable instance of this is the way the Nene, the Ouse, the Granta, the Little Ouse and the Wissey formerly entered the sea at Wisbech. Castle Rising was a flourishing port when King's Lynn was a marsh. In the twelfth century four settlements named Wiggenhall stood on the Norfolk marshes. The interesting part of the name is that the *halh* in it meant 'a bend in the coast, or a bay', indicating a pronounced curve in the Wash at that point.

There were few places on the actual coastline of Norfolk suitable for landing an army; but the rivers were a different matter. The groups that collectively became the East Anglians poured into these and evidently liked what they found because they appear to have shown little inclination to stray. At Domesday, Norfolk was the most populous county in England. Perhaps the fact that the East Anglians were so mixed racially – although closely related – meant that they lacked the leadership the Saxons had. So the lively part of the history of East Anglia came with the Danes, who first attacked the east coast of England about 820. Thirty years later they were to be found wintering in Kent, East Anglia and Northumbria. Then in 870 came the wintering at Thetford, from which they distributed over a wide area during the following summer. So in Norfolk, Scandinavian names ending in both -by and -thorp are common, and it seems probable that most if not all of them looked to Thetford for their administration.

In Suffolk the Scandinavian place-names near the mouth of the

Waveney tell their own story, and in Lowestoft we have the interesting Old Danish 'toft', which originally meant a plot of land for a homestead, but in some places seems to have been used for a low hill or tump. Langland in *The Vision of Piers Plowman* writes:

> I saw a tower on a toft:
> A deep dale beneath.

From Lowestoft the Danes worked upsteam to drier land. The Hundred name Thingoe, with Risby (-by at a clearing), shows that there was a Scandinavian colony in the Bury St Edmunds district large enough to have its own thing, or assembly.

In the southern half of Suffolk there were many more points of entry, with the result that the low-lying land between the Alde and the Orwell has many early place-names, not all of them readily explicable. Halesworth was clearly Hael's worth, or clearing, Walberswick (Wahlberht's wick), with wick used for a dairy farm as it was so freely on the Essex marshes. In Saxmundham the 'Sax' is no great problem. It is related to either the Saxon or his sword; but the 'mund' is a curiously common element in East Anglian place-names, and as we cannot be sure what it means we ascribe it to a personal lord. Other places with the same element in their names are Mendham, Mundham, Mundesley, Mendlesham and Mundford. There are various alternative theories for its origin, including 'mound', which does not seem improbable.

Along this part of the Suffolk coast we have the opposite to what was found in the Wash, in that here the land recedes. Dunwich, which in Anglo-Saxon times was the cathedral city of East Anglia, has long been under the sea. With the long shingle spit of Landguard point at Felixstowe we have a corruption of the Anglo-Saxon *lang gara*, *gara* being the same word as gore, a piece of land shaped like a spear, a 'gar'. And having in our hands a spear, what better use could be made of it than to kill the fond belief that Felixstowe takes its name from St Felix, 'the apostle to the East Angles'. It has no connection with him. The earliest form of the name is *Filethstowe*, which means nothing more romantic than 'a place where trees were felled'.

CHAPTER SEVEN

The North Midlands

Lincoln is the starting point for a new approach to local place-names. In the shires of the North Midlands, and progressively as we move into the northern counties of England, Scandinavian influence becomes a major factor, with Danish giving place to Norse when we reach eastern Cumbria. Lincolnshire, the second largest county in England – like Yorkshire, the largest – is divided into three parts: Lindsey, Kesteven and Holland. Lindsey, as a name, is derived directly from the British *Lindon* and is identical with the Welsh *llyn*, 'lake'. It refers to the widening of the Witham as it may still be seen in Brayford Mere. The 'ey' in the name is for island, a reminder that the district was practically enclosed by water before the Fens on the Witham were drained. In Kesteven, the first part is British and related to the Welsh *coed*, 'wood', the second to the Scandinavian *stefna*, 'a meeting', suggesting that the name was intended to indicate a district with a common meeting-place, or an administrative district. Holland is Old English and means 'land on the spur of the hill'.

The Danes were organisers and planners. Unlike the Saxons, who sailed up the rivers and settled on the banks to start their settlements in family holdings, the Danes forged inland – where possible along Roman roads – to occupy towns and stimulate their trade. It is notable that in five of the principal boroughs of these North Midland shires they left the existing names untouched. Only Derby among them received the dignity of the Scandinavian suffix -by. In rural areas it seems probable that the people remained undisturbed so long as they accepted the Danes as a new ruling class.

In their successful assault in the last quarter of the ninth century, the Vikings made their way through to Lincoln, which as *Lindum Colonia* had been the headquarters of the Ninth Legion, and established themselves in strength. From Lincoln they used the existing Roman roads for colonisation by their marching armies in a manner more akin to that of the Romans than to that of any north European race. Proof of this is to be found in the large number of names ending in -by along Ermine Street as it runs south through Kesteven. No doubt Ancaster, 'the Roman fort of Anna', would be used, and the traveller who is attracted by the name into visiting the town will be rewarded by seeing the results of excavations.

To the north of Lincoln we find -by names along the east side of Ermine Street in greater numbers than along the west, except near the mouth of the Trent. An examination of these contributes considerably to an understanding of the general character of the Scandinavian settlement of Lincolnshire, in which, according to Professor Ekwall, their influence on place-names was at its highest. Such an examination certainly establishes that the names ending in -by are earlier than those ending in -thorpe, and that in general the places with -thorpe endings were secondary settlements. We many recall how Tennyson in *The Brook* writes: 'I hurry down . . ., by twenty thorps, a little town, and half a hundred bridges'. The large -thorpes like Scunthorpe, Cleethorpes and Mablethorpe reached their present size in recent times. Scholars can even be so precise as to state that most of the -by endings near Roman roads mark settlements taken over by the Danes in the late eight-seventies. There are seventy of them in the Spilsby area of Lindsey, forty in the Sleaford–Bourne area of Kesteven. Few -by endings in central Lincolnshire have a Danish personal name as prefix. Where they are found they are on the fringes of areas containing many earlier names.

The name Ingleby, found in other counties as well as in Lincolnshire, provokes the question of why the existing Anglian population should have been singled out in this way. This may have been complimentary. As the Scandinavians who settled the North Midlands were Danes, who came from fertile country where the people got their living by dairy farming, they may have settled happily with the Angles, leaving the men of more pioneering spirit to press on. This theory is supported by the number of Scandinavian names near the banks of the Lower Bain and its tributaries to the east. Bain, incidentally, is itself a Scandinavian river name. Another name that commemorates earlier settlers is Spalding, 'dwellers by the ditch', a name that has a twin in Spauwen in Holland.

If we are looking for clues to the progress of the Danish armies we must see that in Nottingham they would find a base as strong as, if not stronger than, their first base at Lincoln. The defensive potential of the rock on which the city stands is immediately apparent. The immense military value of this stronghold during the Danish wars is too long a story to tell here; but Nottingham was bound to become an important administrative centre of the shire system which the Danes so effectively established in these Midland counties. In view of this it may be thought surprising that Nottinghamshire has only twenty-one names ending in -by, against fifty-eight in Leicestershire, and more than two hundred and seventeen in Lincolnshire. The few names ending in -by that are to be found in Nottinghamshire tend to be in small clusters such as we find in the Bassetlaw Wapentake. In fact, most of the Scandinavian settlements in the county seem to have been west of the Trent and near the river. There are few to be found further into the county, and this reference to the Bassetlaw Wapentake may remind us that in Domesday Book the Scandinavian shires, as explained earlier, are not divided into Hundreds but into Wapentakes, a Scandinavian word meaning 'flourishing of weapons in an assembly'. This is a characteristically Viking touch, although Sir Frank Stenton could find 'no essential difference of function between the courts of the Wapentake and those of the Hundred'.

The explanation of the comparative fewness of the -by endings in Nottinghamshire is surely that the county was used in the early stages of Danish occupation as a base for marching armies rather than for settlement. This is supported by the greater number of the later ending, -thorpe, to be found there. Another interesting feature is the number of names with the hard Scandinavian 'k' substituted for the earlier 's' or 'sh'. The most obvious of these is Fiskerton, which was the fishermen's village.

All this goes to show that in Nottinghamshire the Danish culture was superimposed on an earlier one that was already of sufficient strength to resist change for a considerable time. This earlier culture was Anglian. The Angles had come up the Trent valley, and occupied Nottinghamshire in their progress towards Derbyshire and Staffordshire, which were to become the heart of the Mercian kingdom. Their record is to be read in such place-names as Gedling, Walkeringham, Beckingham, Hoveringham and Nottingham itself.

An attractive feature in the place-names of Nottinghamshire is the number that contain descriptive elements. They are found in field-names especially, and I am told that they are common in documents of land title. They include *myrr* 'marsh', *holm* and *ing* 'meadow' and *deill* for a share or strip in the village field. This last example is to be found in the farm name Wandales, which occurs in several places. In it the Scandinavian *deill* is prefixed with 'Wand', signifying a tract of land in which the width of each strip was measured by a long slender rod. The custom of measuring land in this way survived in Nottinghamshire until the eighteenth century, when the wand had a standard measurement of 14ft 6ins.

Another important group that might be more meaningful than is immediately apparent is the one with a Scandinavian personal name before the -ton ending. These occur in areas well settled by the Angles before the Danes came. Thrumpton, two miles from the cremation cemetery at Kingston-on-Soar, is one. The point about them is that when the Danes divided up the county, the new overlord did not impose a -by ending, but was content simply to add his own name to the existing -ton, much as the Normans were to do later. So in Nottinghamshire rather less than normal weight can be attributed to the final element of a place-name in determining its date. It has also to be noted that the five Normantons in the county show that there were also a few Norwegian settlements early enough to be reflected in place-names.

The introduction of a personal name into a place-name often brings out racial differences of basic character. With the Saxons it reflected attachment to the land, with the Normans the use of a personal name was usually manorial. It has been well argued that with the Danes it may have meant no more than that the men who fought under a leader in the army were happy to settle under him when spears were turned into ploughshares, and that nothing more compulsive than simple human loyalty entered into the reckoning. It was suggested earlier that in some places Norman names were introduced to distinguish between several older identical British names. With the Scandinavians the use of personal names in place-names led to repetitions, because they had a habit of giving the same name to many members of a single family, both in its different branches and in different generations. This is said to have been due to a belief that the soul of a person was symbolised in his name, and that by bestowing the honoured name of the departed on a new-born child the spirit of the lost one would enter into the namesake. This led to so much confusion that what are now called 'fun-names' were introduced, many of which are no longer recognisable for what they are, A *ketill* was a round pot. Consequently a round-headed man acquired it as a nickname, and this found its way into such names as Ketsby, Kettleby,

Kettlethorpe and Kedleston. One wonders whether so dignified a person as Viscount Curzon was aware of this when he took Kedleston into his title. Fráni, meaning 'the bright one', is found in Framland, Leicestershire, while birds are commemorated in such names as Walesby in Lincolnshire and Nottinghamshire, from *valr*, 'falcon'; *orre*, 'moor-hen' in Orby, Lincolnshire. Most, however, are satirical. So we have *klakkr*, meaning 'clod', in Claxby, and *Skúma*, 'the squinter', in Scunthorpe, while *Slengr*, 'the idler', gave his name to Slingsby.

To return to the main lines of settlement, Leicestershire followed the same course as Lincolnshire and Nottinghamshire in that it was from the capital and in pockets. The largest proportion of Scandinavian names are in the east and the north-east, and are to be found alongside English names, or even incorporated in them as in Nottinghamshire. In the Wreak valley, within six miles of Melton Mowbray, there are twenty-four names ending in -by; but Scandinavian personal names are just as common with -ton as their suffix. What is even more decisive of Scandinavian influence in the Wreak valley is that a document of 1322 shows that the language of the Danes was still in use in official records there four and a half centuries after the Danish occupation, although by that time Norman influence had given rise to such names as Ashby-de-la-Zouche, in which 'Zuche' means stump.

The main thing to note about the distribution of place-names in the North Midlands is that outside these early settlements made from rivers and Roman roads the area was one vast forest, which was not only heavily wooded, but was subject to the harsh Forest Laws. Even as late as the twelfth and thirteenth centuries there had been little social development in these regions. In fact, it was in the second half of the twelfth century that the Forest Laws operated with their maximum vigour. The forest of Rockingham was bordered by Salcey Forest in Northamptonshire, which has a French name meaning 'willow wood', and Salcey ran across country to Whittlebury. The Saxons established themselves in clearings in what is now Rutland. So we get such names as Lyddington and Uppingham, 'the village of the sons of Uppa'; but there are few names with earlier endings, and Rutland is exceptional among divisions of the Mercian kingdom in that it did not become a 'shire' bearing the name of its principal town. If it had, it would presumably have been Oakhamshire. To the north of the Rutland and Leicestershire forests were the forests of Sherwood and Nottinghamshire and Needwood in Derbyshire extending as far as the Peak. Settlements in all these areas, as Professor

W. G. Hoskins brought out in his *Essays in Leicestershire History*, were both small and late. He shows also that post-Domesday names ending in -cote, -leah and -thorpe, which were secondary to existing settlements along established routes, increased greatly between 1150 and 1300, and that post-Domesday names ending in -leigh at this date are more likely to indicate clearings than woods. But they would be small and occupied by forestry workers.

Staffordshire in this group is, in a sense, the odd man out in that it does not fall into the pattern so far traced, and has strong connections with the counties of the South Midlands; but it figures prominently in the history of the Danelaw. The Angles who came up the Trent through Nottinghamshire made their first settlement at Tamworth, 'the enclosure on the river Tame', a name identical with *Taff* in Wales and Lichfield, 'the field of corpses', which marked the site of the battle in which they conquered the Britons. The king of the Mercian kingdom had his capital at Tamworth; the bishop his seat at Lichfield. When the Danes invaded Mercia, Alfred the Great was able to come to the defence of the natives, and in 878 he made peace with the invaders, dividing Mercia into two parts in a treaty that left Staffordshire to the English and gave Derbyshire and Leicestershire to the Danes. It was this treaty that made Watling Street the western boundary of the Danelaw.

The credit for rescuing east Staffordshire from the Danes belongs to Alfred's daughter, Ethelfleda, 'the Lady of the Mercians', of whom it was written:

> Oh, potent Ethelfleda, terrible to men,
> Whom courage made a king, Nature a queen.

The line of her forts runs from Tamworth, where she died in 922, to Stafford which had previously been called Bethany. The names of the Hundreds of Staffordshire tell their own tale: Pirehill, 'the hill of the pear tree', Totmonslow, the burial mound of Totman, 'the bright and happy fellow'. Another Hundred name is Seisdon, 'the Saxon's hill'. But Staffordshire had closer racial relationship with the land of the Hwicce to the south and west. Wichnor, for example, must have derived its name from the Hwicceans of Worcestershire. Staffordshire is, however, closely linked with Derbyshire, where there is little place-name evidence of Scandinavian settlement except in the Repton Hundred, which borders Leicestershire. There are only nine places with names ending in -by in the whole of the county and none in the Peak. Rowland is the only village west of the Derwent that has a Scandinavian name, although the Booths in the Edale valley, which originated as shelters for cattle, may indicate a Scandinavian system of farming. But Derbyshire is no less remarkable for its lack of early Anglo-Saxon names. It has no name ending in -ingas or -ingham, although Derby, no less than Leicester and Nottingham, was a thriving mercantile centre before the Danes arrived. Again, the explanation is the heavily wooded character of the region, giving it many names with -worth endings: Buxworth, Charlesworth, Chisworth, Hollingworth, and Ludworth to the north-west of Kinder Scout, in all of which 'worth' meant an enclosure round a homestead.

Some of Derbyshire's most fascinating names are derived from the long history of its lead mines. Such names as Venture, Goodluck, Hark Rake and Hazard are reminders of the risks attached to the industry. The veins of lead were called rakes and live on in such names as Dirtlow Rake and Long Rake, and in Leadmill Bridge at Hathersage and Leadmines Farm at Elton. Domesday Book records three lead mines at Wirksworth and single mines at Crich, Bakewell, Ashford and Matlock. The name 'King's Field' for the whole area between Wirksworth and Castleton is derived from the right to a royalty on all ore obtained from this area. Among peculiarly local names the most interesting is Bole Hill, which occurs almost as frequently in Derbyshire as 'hammer' does in Sussex. It refers to the primitive hearths, called boles, where the lead-smelting was done, the lead being brought to them by trains of pack horses. There were shallow holes excavated in the brow of a hill facing the prevailing wind. A popular reminder of the industry is the inn sign, 'The Pig of Lead'.

It must not be thought that because the Anglo-Saxon settlement came late, and the density of the surrounding forests precluded early cultivation of the valleys, that the social history of the whole of Derbyshire began late. Far from it. Some of the finest stone circles in England are to be found there. Near Hartington is Aborlow, at Dove Holes near Chapel-en-le Frith is the 'Bull Ring', and Derbyshire caves have yielded many Neolithic and Bronze Age objects of importance. In Mam Tor, the most impressive Iron Age hill-fort in the southern Pennines, we have the Celtic word that occurs also in Mansfield, Nottinghamshire, a hill name that is the source of the Irish word for breast and the Welsh *mam* for mother. On Hathersage Moor, to the east of Mam Tor, is Carl Wark, in which the second element is from *weorc*, 'fort', and the first element suggests that it was the fort of free peasants. Hathersage is in a valley under a steep ridge called Millstone Edge, a reminder that the faulted sides of the Pennines are called Edges. And far from agriculture coming late to this hill country, we have impressive evidence of the use made of narrow ledges or lynchetts on to which from prehistoric times fertile soil was washed down from the rocks.

The name 'Tor' has just been mentioned. This is another instance of strong Celtic influence in the place-names of Derbyshire, which is the only county away from the extreme south-west of England where it is found. In Mellor, a name found also in Lancashire, we have the Welsh *meol* 'bare' found in Malvern, and in Dinting the Old Irish word *dinn* for 'hill'.

In the limestone hills between the Manifold Valley and the Hamps is Muden, where a group of barrows contain evidence of Anglo-Saxon pagan burials, while in the Peak District, the Old English *hlaw*, meaning burial mound or hill, occurs in about seventy place-names, of which thirty are associated with burial mounds, and if we note how many of these 'lows' occur on the limestone plateau near ancient trackways we are led to the conclusion that they mark sites occupied by Anglians making their way north from the Trent valley in the late sixth or early seventh century.

The Romans found a series of prehistoric tracks in the Peak District and used them as the basis for their own network of communications; but only at Little Chester, Brough and Melandra, near Glossop, did they build forts. These were connected by roads that ran through Buxton to Manchester. The mystery of why there were so few Roman forts in an area so rich in metal remains unsolved. The lead mines of Dovedale, near Matlock, were certainly important in Roman times, and with four roads converging on it, Buxton, where the virtues of the mineral springs were discovered, was an important centre.

Following the Roman withdrawal, a cloud descends on Derbyshire's history; but interest picks up again in the many place-names associated with paganism. Drakelow in the south of the county means 'dragon's mound', suggesting that there was a myth about a dragon connected with the place, and Drakelow is only about a mile away from the heathen cemetery at Stapenhill, near Burton-on-Trent in Staffordshire, a county with more than one town associated with heathen worship. The most notable of these are, of course, Wednesbury and Wednesfield, so obviously associated with the worship of Woden. At Wednesbury the church is built on an earthwork.

But Derbyshire's isolation did not continue long after the Roman era. The Peak was brought into Mercia by Penda in 626, and for a time its central geographical position gave Derbyshire eminence, if not pre-eminence, in the Mercian kingdom; but two place-names remind us that the Danish invaders destroyed some of the region's dignity. Repton in Derbyshire shared with Tamworth in Staffordshire the status that went with a place of royal residence. It was also the site of a monastery destroyed by the Danes, which may remind us that despite Derbyshire's pagan connections it is also a county outstanding for its early examples of Christian art. Saxon crosses stand at Wirksworth, Bakewell, Bradbourne and Eyam, and others showing Scandinavian influence in Dovedale, at Norbury, Derby and Wilne, 'the island of the willows'.

At the Norman Conquest Derbyshire, still hemmed in by forests and moorland, can have had little attraction except for sport. Darley, two miles north of Derby, was 'the wood frequented by deer'. So the county was given to a favourite, Henry de Ferrers, whose grandson was to be created Earl of Derby. But Henry de Ferrers did not think highly enough of the gift to build himself a castle there. He built it at Tutbury in Staffordshire. Derbyshire nevertheless did get its castles. The first was built at Castleton, on a tongue of land projecting into the Peak, and its builder's name, William Peveril, was to find a place in literature when Sir Walter Scott made use of it for a Carolean romance. Another castle was built on a hill at Bolsover, 'the bullock pasture'. It is to be noted that 'castle' in place-names is French. The Newcastles as well as the Castletons are all post-Conquest.

Derbyshire was unfortunate in that it failed to find favour with either the Benedictines or the Cistercians. Its only monastic landowner was the abbot of Burton; but small religious houses were founded at Derby, Darley, Calle, which was transferred to Repton, and nearly fifty monastic granges were established in the Peak after the middle of the twelfth century. The designation of these small foundations as granges indicates that they were granaries. There were no fewer than nine of them in the Hundred of Wirksworth subject to Papal taxation. Several belonged to Darley Abbey, others to the wealthy Premonstratensian abbey at Welbeck in Nottinghamshire.

So Derbyshire's life, in so far as there was any unity in it, was primarily sporting. The Peak itself was a royal forest, and within the shire there were more than fifty smaller forests. But it had one surprising link with the Church, and that was with the martial Church of the North. Henry I granted the church at Melbourne to the Bishop of Carlisle as part of the endowment of the See. As Carlisle was then subject to Scottish raids, the bishop built himself a palace at Melbourne and held ordinations there.

That Derbyshire should have had a link with Carlisle at so early a date seems surprising until we realise how the English road system was emerging; but this only becomes fully plain to us when we move north-west into Cheshire. This proud county as we have it now derives its name from Chester, and the importance of Chester is shown in that while there are many towns in England with 'chester' as part of their name, there is only one that bears the designation unadorned and unqualified. Chester achieved this unique position by virtue of having five important Roman roads converging on it, and if we follow these out of the city gates to their several destinations we see that it was clearly from Chester that the Romans planned the subjection of the rebellious North. The advantages of these communications remained after the Romans had withdrawn, bringing prosperity to Chester in peace and strategic importance in war until the city became the great stronghold of Mercia, and the last town in England to acknowledge the finality of the Norman Conquest.

After William the Conqueror had sent his legionaries to harry the stiff-necked people of the North-East of England in the manner to be described later, with the object of devastating the entire region between York and Durham, he turned west to wreak his vengeance on Chester; but he quickly saw that this was not a city to be destroyed and forgotten. So he built his castle on the mound that had been fortified by Ethelred the Unready and established the city as a feudal capital. Like Lancaster it became the seat of an earldom with palatinate privileges.

But the prosperity of Chester was not necessarily reflected in the country surrounding it. Towards the sea lay the forest of Wirral, extending from the Dee to the Mersey, with the forests of Delamere to the north-west and Macclesfield beyond it forming an impenetrable barrier beween Cheshire and Derbyshire. When the Normans laid waste the whole of the land between Chester and the Pennines the population of the Forest of Macclesfield was almost completely exterminated and there was little recovery for centuries. Only along the valleys of the Dee, the Weaver, the Cowy, and the western plain – always subject to raids by the Welsh – did any considerable population survive in Cheshire outside the city itself. The land was poor, the people backward, giving rise to the saying: 'Cheshire born and Cheshire bred; strong i' th' arm, weak i' th' head'.

The exceptions were the 'wiches': Northwich, Middlewich and Nantwich, towns that derive their name from *wych*, meaning 'rock salt'. The discovery of the large deposit of salt lying in the stratified rocks of the old redstone of this region was made by the Romans. It extends over a field about thirty miles long and fifteen miles wide along the valley of the Weaver, a name which aptly means 'winding river', and was probably applied earlier to at least part of what is now the Mersey.

As elsewhere, early names survive in Cheshire along the rivers, with a crop of later Saxon names as we move inland, most of which end in -ton. Cheshire has four Astons and five Suttons. But in the Wirral we get such Scandinavian names as Kirby, Raby, Frankby and Greasby, reminders of the Norwegians who arrived at the beginning of the tenth century. Racially the county is more mixed than most, particularly if we take into account that Lancashire south of the Ribble was included in Cheshire at Domesday.

CHAPTER EIGHT

North West England

LANCASHIRE · WESTMORLAND · CUMBERLAND

From Derbyshire to the Tyne Valley we have the Pennines, a sprawling mass of mountain ranges split by the Aire Gap into two approximately equal parts, with river systems forming dales that give a distinctive character to each division and sub-division. As elsewhere, the hills and rivers bear names that record the progress of the folk who settled them. In Lancashire the Brigantes were the freemen of the hills, the Segantii the 'dwellers in the land of many waters'. Both were difficult to dislodge. In the north of what constituted the county of Lancashire until the nineteen-seventies the mountains billow out to the coast north of Morecambe Bay, and there the rivers are trapped in rocky fastnesses to form the lakes of England's most romantic landscape. Between these and the Derbyshire Peak stretch vast areas of infertile country that are now covered with the teeming boroughs of industrial Lancashire – the Lancashire the southerner believes is all there is to the county. West of these bewildering towns lies the Fylde, which is the Old English word for 'plain', forming the western part of Amounderness, a name derived from Old Norse and meaning the headland of one *Agmundre*. In this part of Lancashire we also have one of the few names signifying early Saxon settlement in Pilling, lying across the Wyre from Fleetwood. And Wyre is a British river name meaning 'winding stream'. So in Lancashire we have the variety of racial elements we found in Derbyshire and Cheshire, surviving as in the other two counties as a result of the remoteness of the terrain to early settlers and its infertility.

These factors did not deter the Romans, and it is to them that we owe the opening up of the region and its gradual struggle towards individual identity. Their starting point was Chester. From that ancient stronghold they constructed three main roads through what was to become Lancashire: one through Manchester to York, another from Manchester through Blackburn, Clitheroe and the Forest of Bowland to lead eventually to Kirkby Lonsdale, a third through Warrington and Wigan to Lancaster. From these they hoped to encompass the region and bring about the subjugation of the North. The fortified sites from which this assault was to be organised were probably Manchester, Ribchester, and Lancaster. From these they could command the Dee and Mersey estuaries, and by constructing roads up the valleys of the Lune and the Ribble they could plan the control of north Lancashire, while from Kirkby Lonsdale they could attack Westmorland. Military stations were established at Warrington, Wigan, Blackburn, Preston and Clitheroe – all of which were to develop into towns of administrative importance, and become chartered boroughs at early dates. In view of its strategic position it may be thought odd that Clitheroe did not develop to the size achieved by the others. After all, Lancaster was an outpost geographically, while Clitheroe might be thought to hold the key to progress towards both Westmorland and Yorkshire. The explanation of its failure to do so is undoubtedly in the forests that enveloped it, and it is in these that many of Lancashire's most characteristic place-names are found. They were examined by Professor Ekwall, who found in them valuable evidence of the survival of a Celtic population on the fells, and of the persistence of ancient ways of life in the woodlands.

The largest areas of forest were in Blackburnshire. The forest of Wyresdale merged into that of Quernmore, the moor where the millstones were cut, and Pendle Forest with its Celtic hill name, while Pendle ran cheek by jowl with Bowland. In all, these forests extended over an area of seventy-six square miles and contained such names as Billington, where the battle of Billangahoh was fought in 798. The same battle gives us the place-name Langho, and it may be that two mounds near Hacking were where Alric and some of his men were buried. Hacking is near Ribchester, where the most impressive Roman remains to be found in Lancashire may be seen. And nearby, incidentally, is the name Dunkenhalgh, which is simply Duncan's *halh* or *haugh*, but illustrates how an element common throughout England has a different meaning in the North from the one it bears in the South. In the South it means 'nook, recess, or small valley'; in the North, as *haugh*, it is a flat piece of alluvial land on a river bank. Haighton is the -ton on the haugh. As valley and ravine names change so much from one district to another we do not need to do more than comment on the use of 'Trough' for valley in the

Trough of Bowland and Trawden, and the frequent occurrence of that evocative name 'clough' for ravine, a name that fascinated the poet-priest Gerard Manley Hópkins while he was at Stonyhurst.

Other forest names are Boarsgreaves, Hogshead, Wolstenholme, Sowclough, Swinstone and Wolfenden. But the towns did develop, and many of them bear Saxon names of the middle period, and are earlier than those with descriptive terminals, like -field, -hurst, and so forth, although we have some of these, such as 'hurst' in Stonyhurst just mentioned. They lie to the south and west of the fells, and are among Lancashire's oldest parishes. Among them are Heysham, Halton, Preston, Kirkham, St Michael's on Wyre, Poulton-le-Fylde, Garstang, Lytham, Whalley (where there are three Saxon crosses), Croston, Eccleston, Wigan, Winwick (where there is the fragment of a Saxon cross), Warrington, Manchester and Rochdale. All, it may be noted, are within easy reach of rivers and occupy the kind of land the Saxons welcomed. In view of the rapid development of the Lancashire of the Industrial Revolution, and of the Coketowns of *Hard Times* (Preston), it may surprise many to learn that in this region there were at least twelve parish churches at Domesday, although there was still no county of Lancaster to be credited with them.

The county of Lancashire was formed in 1169 by detaching the district of Cartmel – from the Norse *Kart-melr*, meaning 'sandbank by rocky ground' – and the district of Amounderness from Yorkshire, and uniting them with the southern region, which was held by the Crown, and was part of the great earldom of Chester. Before the Conquest the heavily wooded country north of Morecambe Bay and bordering it had been of little use for anything except sport; but the trees had been cleared with such vigour by the monks of the Cistercian abbey of Furness, founded by King Stephen in 1127, that Henry II was persuaded to recognise Lancaster as the head of a new county, bestowing royal status upon it by conferring the earldom on his son, John. To compensate for the sparse population of the county and the vast extent of its marshes and forests, Henry gave his son regal rights within the shire. The star of Lancaster was at last in the ascendant. In 1352 Edward III introduced into England the noble title of Duke and made Lancashire a Duchy, raising it at the same time to the status of a County Palatine, with the right to appoint a chancellor and judges, which were to include, when the office was created, Justices of the Peace. Since that time, woe betide any man who in giving the Loyal Toast at a function in the county fails to add: 'Duke of Lancaster'.

In a sense, the Crown might be said to have held together racial groups as different in many respects as some that were held together under the Crown in the Commonwealth of Nations. Lancashire extended into the Lake District on the Furness side of Morecambe Bay, and the inhabitants of that part of the county had little in common with the people of Merseyside or Manchester. But the traditional loyalty of all Lancastrians to the Crown gave them a unity that people from other counties have often failed to understand. Now alas! Lancashire has lost some of its finest scenery with the restoration of Furness to Cumbria. It has, however, gained some beautiful villages in Bowland from the West Riding of Yorkshire, and from the place-name point of view these belong to the region planned by the Romans and defended by the Celts in a way they could not really belong to the region east of the Pennines.

Westmorland always did belong to Cumbria, from which it was severed, and to which it has now been restored. It was formed out of the baronies of Appleby and Kendal, which is why the two towns are regarded by many as twin capitals. The region has never been rich. It had no wealthy monasteries or large settlements; but it was a peaceful region, enjoying protection from the Picts by virtue of having Cumberland and Northumberland to withstand the first assaults. In consequence of this relative security its people developed the thrifty and modestly prosperous characteristics that appealed so much to Wordsworth. It became the land of the 'dalesmen' to a degree not equalled by either the people of Cumberland or even of Yorkshire in the proud days before the Industrial Revolution reached that county. This is largely because the Westmorland dalesmen never came under the heel of feudal lords. They were free to toil long days cultivating their small holdings for their own benefit. Their occupations were almost entirely pastoral, even although the men were liable for military service if the Picts threatened security. The name 'dalesman' may not come from the dales they lived in, but from 'delen', to divide. These shrewd men appreciated the value of private property and divided their land into estates, which gave them the alternative name of 'statesmen'.

So in Westmorland we look for names not so much of castles that give us clues to martial traditions, although there were castles, like those at Kendal and Brougham, defending mountain passes and associated with such great names as the Cliffords of Appleby. Instead, there were historic peles that became manor houses, and homes of such families as the

Flemings. Sizergh and Levens are mansions extended from pele towers. Most of the best known family-names of Westmorland are those of men who sprang from industrious peasant and modest parson stock. They are again the names that Wordsworth delighted to honour. Even the names of the mountain passes do not carry the ring of some in other parts. There is Kirkstone, for example, meaning 'church stone'. Why, we do not know. Perhaps a tired traveller rested after the long climb out of Ambleside and imagined he saw the outline of a church steeple in the fissures of the rock face before him. Dunmail Raise does celebrate a battle. Raise is from the Norse word for cairn, and Dunmail is the name of the last king of Cumbria. As he fell here after being conquered by Edward in 946, no doubt the cairn was built to mark the spot where he was supposed to have fallen. Wrynose Pass again provokes a fanciful explanation. The name is found in both Cumberland and Lancashire. It means 'the stallion's neck of land'. If we turn to the lakes themselves, Grasmere is simply what it appears to be, the lake with the grassy banks, Rydal is 'the valley where the rye was grown', Coniston is 'the king's ton'.

But if Westmorland place-names evoke few recorded heroic memories, the wilder parts of the county are covered with prehistoric relics, especially along the range of limestone hills near Orton, 'the ton of the Black Cock'. Long barrows containing burnt bodies have been found at Crosby Garrett and Raisett Pike, and round barrows at Ashfell, Kirkby Stephen, Askham, Brackenber Moor, Crosby Garrett, Crosby Ravensworth, Dufton Church, Gamelands, Orton, Great Ashby Scar, Ravenstonedale, Shap, Raftland Forest and Warcop. Megalithic Circles are to be seen at Crosby Ravensworth, Gamelands, Gunnerkeld, Karl Lofts and Guggleby Stone (near Shap), Lowther Scar, Moor Divock and Ravenstonedale. There are twelve sites of prehistoric villages and, in addition to these, there are twenty-four earthworks, including one called 'King Arthur's Round Table'. Hardly a valley in the Lake District lacks evidence of being inhabited from the late Iron Age onwards.

An interesting feature of these ancient relics from the place-name point of view is their descriptive nature. The Crosbys are -bys with crosses. Ravensworth is the worth of someone known as Raven, presumably because he had raven-black hair, like the Black Cock of Orton. Ashby, Ashfell, Askham, were all places where ash trees grew. Brackenber contains bracken; Dufton was the Dove -ton. The short, uninspiring name of Shap actually refers to a ruined pre-historic stone circle.

It first appeared as Yhep. The change to Shap has an analogy in the Shetlands, with a common element which is believed to mean 'heap'. All these bring out the difference referred to earlier between the imaginative Scandinavian and the earthy Saxon character. The frequency of names containing 'ash' reminds us of a passage in Wordsworth's *Guide to the Lakes*: 'This sylvan appearance is heightened by the number of ash-trees planted in rows along the quick fences, and along the walls, for the purpose of browsing the cattle at the approach of winter. The branches are lopped off and strewn upon the pastures; and when the cattle have stripped them of the leaves, they are useful for repairing the hedges or for fuel.'

The glacial rocks of Cumbria give us a sense of the romance of Creation. The Norse and Danish invaders did not establish a village pattern in the way the Saxons did. Despite the fertile nature of the soil away from the mountains, there are few names denoting Danish occupation. They include Appleby, Kirkby Thore, Kirkby Lonsdale, Kirkby Stephen, Temple Sowerby, Thrimby, and Ashby or Askaby. Bannisdale is interesting as an example of Scandinavian addiction to bynames, or nicknames. Bannis was 'the man who curses'.

Directly related to the sheep-rearing in the Lake District was the cloth production on which Kendal flourished by producing a coarse cloth called Kendal Green. Several place-names in Kendal bear evidence of this. Littehouse (1469 ref.) was a dye house, Walke Mylne (1537) was a fulling mill, Tenterfield, Tenterbank, Tenterground, etc. all refer to places where the cloth was stretched on a tenter frame. In 1582 the burgesses of Kendal ordered a watch to be kept on tenters. Another apparent association with local employment is Hayclose, 'the Hay of Kirkby Kendal', which was first referred to in the thirteenth century. It was, in fact, a hunting park on the hills to the east of Kendal Castle.

Kendal was originally Kirkby Kendal, and it is interesting to see how many of the Westmorland towns were developed from Church villages that became market towns and centres of large parishes: Kirkby Lonsdale, Kirkby Stephen, Kirkby Thore. Many of these Kirkbys must owe their origin to the mission of St Cuthbert. Appleby, the county town, must have begun with the establishment of a farmstead with an apple tree; but it became the head of the barony of the Cliffords. Brough, from *burh*, 'fortification', was a Roman fort that became the site of a mediaeval castle. Tebay, 'Tibba's water meadow', has a castle green at Old Tebay, and that exciting name Gaisgill, 'ravine of the wild geese', is found at Whitby, in Northumbria, and in the West Riding of Yorkshire. How depressing, however, to find it in Crosby Ravensworth ascribed to an association with the local gallows!

The importance of the county for defence is shown in the number of prehistoric sites and Roman stations, some of which were succeeded by Norman or mediaeval castles. So Westmorland is a most rewarding hunting ground for the local historian. Its ancient sites have not been obliterated by the plough or by industrial development. Its stone circles, earthworks, prehistoric encampments and entrenchments are still to be seen, often associated with place-names that indicate defensive enclosures, such as Low Green, Ewe Close, and Ewe Locks in Crosby Ravensworth, 'Raven's farmstead with crosses'. At Coneybed in New Hutton the earthwork must have become a rabbit warren. Gamelands in Orton was the site of a stone circle which someone must have thought was where games were played. Perhaps they were. We may be sure that the cockpit in Barton was used for cock-fighting.

Old English settlements are comparatively few in Westmorland, but not unimportant. They bear such -ham names as Heversham and Brougham. The -tons include Bolton, Burton, Clifton, Dalton, Dufton, Hutton, Langton and Preston. Most of them lie in the valleys of the Kent and the Lune, or on the sunny side of the Eden. When we turn to the hills in the Lake District we find that few are named on maps earlier than the eighteenth century. Names like Great Gable, Old Man, Saddleback and Wetherlam are late.

In several names Viking customs and superstitions are reflected, as in Hoff Lunn, from the Old Norse *hof*, meaning 'heathen temple', and *lundr*, 'grove, grove offering sacrifice', while witchcraft is suggested by the name Trough Gill, 'the troll's gill', in Cleburn.

French names appear after the Norman Conquest in Mountjoy, Beacham, Bewley Castle – the residence of the Bishops of Carlisle. Countess Pillar at Brougham, and Lady's Pillar, Mallerstang, are reminders of the influence in the seventeenth century of Lady Anne Clifford, Countess of Pembroke, who at Brougham erected a pillar 'for a memorial of her last parting in this place with her good and pious mother'. Hartshorn Tree at Brougham recalls the story of the removal by vandals of 'one of those hartshorns . . . set up in the year 1333 at a general hunting, when Edward Baliol, then king of Scots, came into England by permission of Edward III . . . the said king hunted a great stag which was killed near the said oak tree. In memory whereof the horns were nailed to it, growing as it were naturally in the tree, and have remained there ever since, till in the year 1648 one of these horns was broken down by some of the army'.

To the historian, Lady Anne Clifford casts her shadow over the region as surely as does Wordsworth. It was she who restored the castles of Pendragon, Lammerside, Brough, Appleby, and Brougham.

Pendragon Castle, incidentally, derives its name from the mediaeval Arthurian romances in which King Uther Pendragon was the father of King Arthur. The local tradition is that Pendragon sought unsuccessfully to fortify the castle by diverting the Eden round it, hence the local proverb: 'Let Uther Pendragon do what he can, Eden will run where Eden ran'. The castle controlled Mallerstang Forest and the trade route into Yorkshire.

While Cumberland and Westmorland achieve unity as Cumbria, there are marked differences between their most characteristic place-names. In Westmorland, British place-names are comparatively rare. In Cumberland they again become numerous; partly, no doubt, as the result of the conquest of the region by the Britons of Strathclyde in the ninth century after the collapse of the Northumbrian kingdom. But as the number of early Anglian names is also small, we may suspect that the British in Cumberland were never dislodged to any great extent. We need to bear in mind also that the Northumbrians had made great progress in Cumbria by the end of the first quarter of the seventh century. Their influence extended to the Solway, and Carlisle remained under Northumbrian control for centuries. The surrounding countryside would not attract the Angles any more than it did the Danes, except in the valleys.

When the Danes arrived in the east, they made their way through the Pennine Gap to settle the eastern fringe of the Lake District. Their villages are still characterised by wide greens, and the change from one tradition to another can come quite suddenly in touring the Lake District. Take, for example, the foot of Ullswater and contrast it with Ennerdale, twenty miles away. On the one hand, Ullswater is an extension of the Eden valley, Ennerdale is related to the Cumberland Plain and the Irish Sea. Great Gable and Kirk Fell (Kirk here meaning 'under', not 'church') have always been effective barriers. As elsewhere, Celtic names survive in the hills and streams of the Lake District. We notice them in Cocker, from a word meaning 'crooked'; Derwent, meaning 'river where oaks were common'; Eden, which has a counterpart in Merioneth and means 'gushing', while Esk is identical in meaning with Exe. What is noteworthy is that the river names of Westmorland are much less Celtic than those of Cumberland. Of the eighteen important river names in Westmorland, only seven or eight are definitely of Celtic origin. As we should expect, there is much more evidence of Celtic survival when we move towards the mountains. Near the Roman fort at Threlkeld the name Blencathra is evidence of Celtic survival. The first part of the name is the Welsh *blaen*, meaning top, and shows that a Celtic-speaking community held on to the Threlkeld enclosure, and in Threlkeld we have a mingling of Celt and Viking, with the Viking introducing a superstitious element in that Threlkeld means 'the thralls' spring'. Glen in Glencoyne, near Ullswater, corresponds with the Celtic word for valley, and the Celtic 'pen', meaning 'head or summit', which appears in both Penruddock and Penrith, has the same meaning as in Pendle Hill, Lancashire. If these Celtic elements are seen to diminish as we move farther north, as they do, the explanation must be that the mountainous land approached from the upper dales was sparsely populated until the Norwegians arrived in the tenth and eleventh centuries.

The two important areas of British settlement in Cumberland are on the fringes. One is on the foothills of the region drained by the Eamont, the other between the Ellen and the Derwent, where we have Blindcrake, 'the rocky summit', Redmain, 'the fort of the stones', and Gilcrux, 'retreat by a hill'.

The reason for the comparative scarcity of British, or Celtic, names in Westmorland is quite simply the extent of the Anglian and Scandinavian settlements, which either obliterated the earlier names or changed them beyond recognition. There is clear evidence for the survival of the Britons at Cartmel in Cark and Blenket, and nearby at Walton; but the explanation of this pocket is to be found in the mediaeval *History of St Cuthbert*, in which it is stated that the district was given by Ecgfrith, king of Northumbria (670–685), to St Cuthbert for the establishment of a monastery, the grant including 'Cartmel and all the Britons with it'. From this we may conclude that the Britons would live on in a subject position after the Anglian invasion. But it does look as though the Anglians took most of the best land near the rivers and pushed the Britons towards the hills as elsewhere. The Danes did not settle to any great extent in Westmorland. Of the -by endings in Domesday Book there are only sixteen in Westmorland against fifty-six in Cumberland.

Bede is our best authority for the Anglian settlement of the North West. He tells us that the frontiers of Northumbria extended over the Pennines; but that they made no attempt to settle the mountain fastnesses, they merely encircled them. So we get -ham terminals in the Eden valley and on the coastal plain of north Cumberland. Much more numerous, which is again what we should expect, are the later -tons. We find them in the Penrith district, in Bampton and Stainton in the Lowther valley, and they are, of course, common in the fertile country round Kendal, which was settled from the rivers that flow into the Kent estuary.

Before going on to consider the effect of the Norse infiltration, it may be thought worthwhile to insert a note about the effect on the place-names of the North of the remarkable mission of St Ninian early in the fifth century, of St Kentigern (or St Mungo), the Apostle to the Strath-clyde Britons, in the sixth century and, above all, of St Cuthbert. The churches at Caldbeck, Castle Sowerby, and Crosthwaite (the mother church of Keswick) are all dedicated to him, as are several others in Cumberland. Close by the churchyard at Castle Sowerby is the well in which he baptised his first converts. This became a place of pilgrimage and led to Castle Sowerby achieving an honoured name which by Scan-dinavian influence was conferred on a family as well as on the place. Crosthwaite became an interesting name in that it combined the mem-ory of the cross set up by St Kentigern with the Scandinavian 'thwaite'. The church at Crosthwaite, later Keswick, became the minster, or mother church, from which chapels of ease were founded to serve all the northern dales of the Lake District, thus contributing greatly to the strength of the Christian character that became so marked a feature of Lake District communities. One of the few dates in the early history of Cumberland that we can be sure of is 573, the date of the battle that established the British Kingdom of Strathclyde, and it was in that same year that St Kentigern preached to the people near Carlisle.

The Norwegians came in some time between 899, the year of King Alfred's death, and 915. So we may take 910 as the approximate date when the Vikings sailed up the Solway and sacked Carlisle. They came in from Ireland and made their way up the valleys into the central fastnesses, climbing the Roman roads to the moors on which their sheep could graze, because they were predominantly shepherd stock. We can follow their progress in place-names up other valleys as well as the Sol-way. Kendal was Kirkby Kendal for centuries, Oxenholme contains the

Old Norse *holmr*, 'an island or water meadow', Sizergh contains the Irish-Norse *erg*. Penetrating into Borrowdale at the heart of the Lake Country we find the Old Norse word for a clearing, *thwaite*, on every hand. Honister Pass has the same derivation as Hunstaad, which is still found on the map of Norway. So complete was the taming of this wild country by British, Anglian and Norse settlers that, contrary to the beliefs of Wordsworthian romantics, the landscape is nowhere untouched by man, although it is obviously far less man-made than that of the South.

For place-name elements giving a clue to the form of government in this Scandinavian region we look for the word 'thing', a council. In documents relating to Swindale, a lonely valley among the Shap fells, we find Thengeheved, the first element in which is clearly 'thing'. This may well have been the site of the local open parliament. The word means 'the council place at the head of the valley'. Ekwall believed that the name Coniston meant 'the king's settlement', from the Old Norse *Kunungstun*. He says: it 'possibly preserves the memory of a small Scandinavian mountain kingdom'.

The introduction by the Scandinavians of names that describe the character of the places in which they settled suggests that they had a strong attachment to the kind of country they came from, and when they found familiar topographical features in the new territory, they gave them the names they had known in their homeland. It is from this characteristic that we are able to distinguish between the places settled by the Danes and those settled by the Norwegians. The Norwegians looked especially for streams in which they could fish, and mountain pastures for their sheep, close to sheltered nooks where they could milk a few cows. They also liked to be near mountain passes through which they could ride out on the backs of their ponies. The clearings on which they built their farmsteads, usually with dwelling and cattle-stalls under one roof, were where we now find the -thwaites. Their barns they called lathes, their summer pastures -saeters, as we have it in Seatoller, their mountain sheds they called scales. To them an enclosure near home was a garth, an orchard an outgarth. So in the small mountainous region of the Lake District and the North Pennines we have such names as Tilberthwaite Ghyll, near Coniston, and Watendlath in the Derwent Valley. When they accepted Christianity the Danes incorporated -kirk into their place-names to commemorate their conversion.

With the Normans came a different kind of settlement. The free spirit of the North became subject to feudal lords, and unashamedly French names, like Egremont from Aigremont, were introduced. In most, however, the final element was left undisturbed, with a French element introduced in front of it. The villages themselves took a new form.

In contrast to the dispersed Norwegian settlements and the Anglian settlements round a small village green, villages were rebuilt with compact lanes, or streets, in triangular formation converging on a castle. There are many such places round Carlisle, where Norman influence was strongest. Alongside the estates belonging to the monasteries founded by the Normans were the sporting estates of the barons, perpetuated in the names of privately owned forests, such as Copeland Forest, which belonged to the barony of Copeland; Grisedale, Thornthwaite, Fawcett, Sleddale – all forests under the control of the barony of Kendal and subject to the restrictions of Forest Laws. Happily the sporting spirit that inspired the feudal lords ran through the veins of the forest workers and farm labourers who occupied their cottages, so the heads of families like the Lowthers were regarded as chieftains rather than oppressors, which explains why, even in industrialised Lancashire, 'Old John of Gaunt, Time honoured Lancaster', remained a rallying call for centuries.

CHAPTER NINE

North East England

YORKSHIRE · COUNTY DURHAM
NORTHUMBERLAND

East of the Pennines was the Saxon kingdom of Northumbria, a region richer and more thickly populated than the western kingdom of Strathclyde. The southern part – Deira – is now Yorkshire, the proud county ruled for centuries by mitred abbots and belted earls. This relative prosperity of the east has been enjoyed throughout history both materially and culturally. Northumbria was the most advanced part of England in learning and religious zeal until the Danes overran it in the ninth century, ransacking and despoiling its monasteries and churches from the Humber to the Forth. It was from the ashes of this devastation that York rose like a phoenix to become a Danish capital of a new shire, the first to be constituted in the North although the actual name does not appear until the fourteenth century. This means that the Danish invasion was the turning point in the history of the North East and largely accounts for the rugged individualism of its people The Danes were followed by the Norwegians, which explains the use of the Old Norse word *land* in Northumberland and Cleveland.

But the place-name history of these counties does not start with the Danes. Roman roads crossed the Pennines out of Lancashire. One intersected the main highway that crossed the Don at Doncaster, then struck north through Tadcaster and Catterick to cross Stainmore, where it linked up with other Roman roads until it reached Hadrian's Wall. York, already important under its earlier name, became the headquarters of a Roman legion and a colonia under Agricola in AD 79 which made it the most important Roman centre in the North of England. The legacy of Roman names, however, is small in Yorkshire. Startford is obviously the ford of the 'street'; but *Eboracum* prefers to be York, although the Archbishop signs himself 'Ebor', *Lavatrae* is content to be

Bowes, and even the Romano-British town of *Isurium Brigantum*, where a Roman temple to Mercury was erected, is happy to call itself Aldborough, 'the old fort'.

An examination of place-names shows that the Angles who settled the area used the Roman roads in the North of England more than the Saxons did in the South. Such names as Bowling, Cowling (locally pronounced Cooling), and Manningham show that there was an early Anglian settlement in Airedale. Near Richmond we have Gilling, a name that occurs again in Ryedale. Others in North Yorkshire are the combination names of Hovingham and Lastingham, and the -ingas tribal name of Pickering. But most of the Anglian settlements in Yorkshire have names ending in -ton or -ley. They are to be found all along the south-facing foothills of the north bank of the Vale of Pickering east of Helmsley.

In the Vale of York Anglian and Scandinavian names are found in roughly equal numbers. Places with -ton as their terminal are widespread around York and over the Wolds. They become less frequent as we move towards the fells and moors, except in pockets, as in the Craven lowlands around Skipton – the Scandinavianised 'sheep town', and Ingleton, both in the west. In the East Riding the Scandinavian occupation must have been so great that earlier place-names, which undoubtedly would be there, disappeared, although there are several hybrid names suggesting villages in which some sort of racial balance was maintained. Perhaps the most interesting of these is Stamford Bridge, the scene of the final defeat of the Danes in 1066. Here the original name was Stanford, 'stone-paved ford', to which *brycg* was added when the bridge was built. Occasionally, Danish influence is to be detected in 'stane' being spelt 'steyn', from the Scandinavian *steinn*. The problems, of course, in the siting of settlements were not entirely racial. In the Wolds, for example, water was a factor. That is why Sledmere, the home of the Sykes family, was established at a place with a name meaning 'pool in the valley', and Fimber at one meaning 'pool amidst the rough coarse grass'.

There had been sporadic raids by the Danes since the middle of the sixth century, but the main landings were during the eighth and ninth. Holderness means 'the ness of the hold', a 'hold' being a high-ranking officer in the Danelaw. From Holderness they spread themselves out until they had occupied the whole of the region that became the East Riding of Yorkshire. Their first communities inland were around Driffield and Beverley, where the land was already in use for dairy farming. From there they crossed the wolds to settle around York and as far west as Ripon, where a number of-ing endings indicate earlier Anglo-Saxon settlement. Harrogate contains the Scandinavian 'gate' for road, and 'Harlow' or 'grey hill', suggesting the 'gate' to the moor where the people had rights of pasturage for cattle.

The Danes would find the fertile valley of the Ouse attractive, and would make their way up its course into the lesser dales that led into the foothills of the Clevelands, 'the hilly district' of the North Riding. In the West Riding they drove the Britons into the fells, where so many early names survive. This would happen at Leeds, for example, which has a name derived from the British *Loidis*, and appears in Bede as the name of a region in the British kingdom of Elmet, a name that has a Welsh counterpart in Elfet in Carmarthenshire, and is perpetuated in the name Sherburn-in-Elmet, near York. From these now industrialised areas the native British would be driven over Ilkley Moor into the rugged dales of Craven, using, no doubt, some of the saltways that gave us such names as Salterforth, near Barnoldswick, and several others that continue to remind us of the tracks along which the pack-ponies carried salt either out of Cheshire or from coastal workings. On the banks of Morecambe Bay are found names like 'Saltcotes', sheds where salt was made, and Saltmarsh at Arnside, Arnbarrow, Birkswood and Askew Green are reminders of an industry that continued on the coast of the Kent estuary from the twelfth century, as we know from the records of tithes paid there.

As Westmorland is pre-eminently the Lake District, Yorkshire is the land of fells and dales. Fell is the Scandinavian word for mountain, dale for deep valleys through which sparkling becks tumble down their rocky courses. Swaledale, the most northern of the five great dales, has a name meaning 'whirling, rushing river'. Each of these five has a ruined abbey to add romance to its scenery and remind us of the power of the Church in the Middle Ages. Two of them, Jervaulx and Rievaulx, have French names translating the names of their streams, the Ure and the Rye, although the Ure failed to give its name to its valley, which became Wensleydale.

In the North Riding are the five lesser dales of Bilsdale, Bransdale, Farndale, Newtondale and Rosedale – a name that is not derived from the flower – not even the white rose of York – but from the Old Norse *hrossa dalr*, 'horse valley', a reminder of the historic connection of the

Yorkshireman with the horse. At one time it was said that if you called for the hostler in the yard behind the principal inn in any town in England a Yorkshireman would appear. Much of the enthusiasm for horse-racing in Yorkshire and other Scandinavian parts of England is derived from the Viking love of the sport. The place-name Hesketh, found in the North Riding, and also in Lancashire and Cumberland, is a compound of the Old Norse *hestre*, 'horse, stallion', and the word for race-course. Other reminders of the horse occur in such names as Studley, 'pasture for horses', and the two names Follifoot and Follithwaite in the West Riding. Foal seems to be an element in these, as the suggestion of breeding is in Studley; but Follifoot could mean 'horse-fight', and horse-fighting was a common sport in Scandinavia.

The -bys and -thwaites of Danish settlement in the North Riding fall into three groups. There is one across Pickering Lythe, South Ryedale and Bulmer Wapentake, another in Whitby Strand and Eskdale, and a third in Cleveland. The point about their location is that they suddenly end and give place to Norwegian names, such as Oswaldkirk, in Upper Ryedale and the country north of Pickering and Kirkbymoorside. In short, they show that the Danes settled along the fertile valleys of the Derwent, the Rye, the Ouse, and in the Vale of York; the Norwegians settled in Upper Ryedale, Cleveland, Teesdale and Richmondshire. Recurring names other than -bys and -thwaites are fascinating. Rudyard Kipling, who came from Yorkshire stock and bore a Yorkshire name, leads us to look for 'hows', from the Norse *haugr*, and Greenhow is there, as we should expect it to be, because Kipling has many claims to be the historian's poet. Among many other hows, or howes, are Burton Howe, Kettle Howe and Three Howes, marking the burial mounds or barrows along Neolithic ridgeways. Another recurring name is Skelton. There are three in the North Riding and others in the West and East Ridings. All are near streams, which suggests that whereas in the South 'Shel' usually indicates a shelving piece of ground, from the Old English *scelf*, in Yorkshire it means 'clatter, splash', from the Old Norse *skellr*. The change is more than the kind of change we get in the substitution of 'k' for 'h', as in Skipton for Shipton; it is another instance of the Scandinavian gift for colourful, descriptive language. The becks run helter-skelter down the dales.

The derivation of the scores of 'kirks' is obvious, but they serve to remind us that the Danes, who came as heathens and destroyed the monasteries and churches, particularly in the year of terror, 867, when

Lastingham and Whitby (both founded in the middle of the seventh century) were destroyed, turned to Christianity when they were themselves defeated. It is all part of the imaginative, superstitious character of the Scandinavians. If they were defeated, they argued, they must have been following false gods, so after Alfdan put them to rout they tried to appease the true God by building churches. Such a name as Kirkby Stephen suggests a personal act of piety. The site of Whitby is as well known as is the fame of Saint Hilda, its abbess, and appears appropriate. Lastingham must always have appeared a strange place for a religious foundation. Bede described it as being built among 'steep and solitary hills, where you would rather look for the hiding place of robbers or the lairs of wild animals than the abodes of men'.

The civilising of these wild moorlands had to await the arrival of the Norsemen, as described by another historian's poet, Sir Walter Scott;

> Beneath the shade the Northmen came,
> Fix'd on each vale a Runic name,
> Rear'd high their altar's rugged stone,
> And gave their gods the land they won,
> Then Balder, one bleak garth was thine,
> And one sweet brooklet's silver line,
> And Woden's Croft did little gain
> From the stern Father of the Stain.

With them the tale of folk settlement as it is reflected in place-names was completed. The Anglo-Saxons had settled on the river banks and in the fertile valleys, where they could grow their crops and lead the kind of life they had led in their homeland, the Danes were less interested in ploughing the land to produce crops than in dairy farming. Finally, the Norse came as shepherds looking for sheep runs and sheltered nooks in mountain passes. Gill, the Norse word for ravine, was introduced in such names as Wemmergill and Scargill. A waterfall was a *foss*, so we got High Force. Rey Cross on Stainmore was given a name derived from the Norse *hreyrr*, a cairn. These names fascinated Dorothy Wordsworth who, in fact, wrote in her Diary: 'a gill . . . is a short and, for the most part, narrow valley, with a stream running through it. Force is a word universally employed in these dialects for waterfall'. She refers also to 'those fissures or caverns, which in the language of the county are called dungeons', as in Dungeon Ghyll.

In Norway the year followed a regular pattern and rhythm of movement. The flocks and small herds were wintered in the valleys and moved into the hills as the pasture extended upwards during the spring and summer months. Outlying farm buildings were called 'scales', and these were sometimes used to identify moors or streams, as in Scales Moor and Scales Beck. These scales would originate in shepherds' huts or sheds. Now they are widespread as names of farms among the fells of Cumbria and the North Riding. The temporary huts on the hillsides used in summer – shielings – frequently have the Old Norse *erg* as part of their name, an 'erg' being a hill pasture, or alternatively 'sett', with the same meaning.

The slope of a hill is often called a bank in the North, from an old Danish word. Firbank in Westmorland and Bank Newton in the West Riding of Yorkshire are examples. But a much older and more characteristic word for a ridge in the North is Rigg. Among the most interesting of the Riggs are Standing Stones Rigg, north-west of Scarborough, Danby Rigg, John Cross Rigg, south-west of Whitby, and Thompson's Rigg, north-east of Pickering, all of which have stone circles along them, raised by the Urn-field folk of the Middle Bronze Age. Wardle Rigg on Goathland Moor first appears in records as Wandel Rigg, which means 'the dale of the Welshmen', as the native British were called, and is therefore another example of the natives retreating into the hills when the Danes attacked.

But not all the original place-names were connected with farming or forestry. In every part of England there are early names connected with mining. In the extreme south-east the metal was iron, in the extreme south-west it was tin. In lovely mellow Gloucestershire there was coal mining in the Forest of Dean, and here in the north-east, where coal mining became so great a force from the days of the Industrial Revolution onwards there are reminders of mining from a very early date. We have Coalgill Syke in Hartley – a syke being a stream – and Coalpit Hill in the lonely moorland parish of Crosby Ravensworth. Reminders of the search for precious metals are found in such names as Silver Keld in Stainmore, 'keld' being a Scandinavian word for 'spring'.

But although the settlement of the mountains by the Norse completed the tale of folk settlement, it did not complete the record of invasion, and no part of England suffered more than the North East. Yorkshire in particular was ravaged as thoroughly in the twelfth century as it had been in the ninth. Villages were burnt by the French as they had been by the Danes. Churches were destroyed throughout the length and breadth of the East and North Ridings. Just as a new Yorkshire rose from the ashes of Viking destruction, a new Yorkshire, still with the old spirit animating it, rose from Norman devastation. At Richmond, Alan of Britanny, the chief of the Norman barons in Yorkshire, built his castle and gave it the name of the French Richemund. Surrounding the castle a district developed that was given the 'shire' name of Richmondshire. Ilbert de Lacy built a castle near a point on the Aire where William I found a broken bridge and called it Pontefract, 'the bridge that is broken'.

Shortly afterwards the monasteries of Evesham and Winchcombe sent monks to restore the religious houses they had read about in Bede. They started at Durham, and from there the inspiration ran south to York, Whitby and Ripon. Then Cistercian monks came over from the Continent to establish Rievaulx. In 1132 brethren of the Benedictine order from the Abbey of St Mary, York, made a new home for themselves in the valley of the Skell near Ripon, and Fountains was founded on plans adapted from St Bernard's Abbey of Clairvaux. Kirkstall was built in the place where foresters had a stall or lodge. Roche Abbey takes its name from the French word for rock. The story goes that the church was built there because pious men wishing to become hermits descried the rough outline of a crucifix on the steep face of the limestone rock there. The abbey of Meaux in the marshes of Holderness takes its name from the birthplace of the first Norman lord of the land on which it stands. And so we might go on. Such foundations as these account for the rich crop of French names found in every part of Yorkshire.

The monasteries of Rievaulx, Fountains, Jervaulx, Kirkstall, Bolton and Sawley are now in ruins, as are the castles of Scarborough, Pickering, Helmsley, Knaresborough, Bolton, Skipton, Pontefract and many others; but the character built up in a hardy people under Norman rule lives on.

The Normans brought the class system as we know it in England, and this has nowhere been more evident in its most vigorous and proud form than in Yorkshire and the counties to the north of it; but it has found expression in an attitude of mind very different from the snobbery engendered in the easier prosperity of the South, which so often reflects the insecurity of sudden accession to wealth. In the South of England those who might be thought to have a right to be proud usually understate their claims. Yorkshiremen could never be accused of this! This northern self-assurance has often led to unpopularity south of the Trent, and such sayings as 'You can tell a Yorkshireman any*where*, but you

can't tell him any*thing*'. In the dales, however, the easy relationship between the landowner and the labourer is something to be respected. A
landowner with a national name might be seen carrying water for a
mason repairing one of his cottages. The relationship is similar to that
seen between a Scottish laird and his gillie.

It is possible that this characteristic in Yorkshire was already there in
undeveloped form under the Danes, who gave nicknames to their -bys.
Blansby is from the nickname Blanda, a stream-name applied to a man
who mixes his drinks; Nafferton is from Nattfari, 'the night traveller',
and provokes speculation as to why he had to travel by night. It may well
be that the earthy humour in such names gives us a clue to the pawky
humour of the Yorkshireman to this day.

A significant feature of Norman names is the appreciation they show
of the beautiful. That is why so many northern names start wtih 'beau' or
'bel'. Butterby in Durham is derived from *beau* and *trouve*. We have Belle
Vues in both Yorkshire and Cumberland. Many of these descriptive
names, however, are reflections of Norman pride rather than of native
appreciation of scenery, which could hardly be expected to develop while
conditions of life remained harsh and the population small. This is not
the place to recount the story of the growth of Yorkshire after the Industrial Revolution. It is not reflected in many place-names; but one example of it may be given. Middlesborough sprang up where only a single
farmhouse stood in 1830, when a syndicate of six Quakers laid out five
hundred acres on the bank of the Tees and started a coal-exporting port.
When the iron industry developed as the result of the mining of ore from
the Cleveland Hills the town grew so rapidly that by 1880 it had a population of fifty-thousand. But we cannot leave Yorkshire without reference
to the woollen industry, and who better to remind us of the source of this
than William Cobbett who, when he caught a glimpse of Holderness,
exclaimed: 'No wonder that the Danes found their way hither so often!'
It gladdened his Radical heart to reflect that 'there were fat sheep then,
as there are now, and these noble churches and magnificent minsters
were reared because the wealth of the county remained in the county,
and was not carried away to the south to keep swarms of devouring tax-
eaters and to cram the maws of wasteful idlers'.

North of the Tees, the 'boiling, surging river', is a territory that still
retains the deep-seated independence that has characterised it throughout its history. It has many British names, but Birling in Northumberland is its only -ingas place-name, and although it has many

Anglian names ending in -ington and -ingham, they are late. Scandinavian names that are so numerous south of the Tees are rare. Of the eight with the -by ending in County Durham, four are in or near Teesdale and suggest a spill-over from Yorkshire. There are no ancient names ending in -by in Northumberland. The 'garth' ending that is common in Yorkshire occurs only once in County Durham. When we consider the extent of the original kingdom and the length of its duration this is remarkable. The name of Northumberland is Scandinavian. It means 'the land north of the Humber', and for many centuries contained the Anglian parts of Scotland as well as the region that became Yorkshire. The Angles were already there in 547, when Ida became their king and built himself a castle at Bamburgh, but the land north of the Tweed was not ceded to Scotland until after the battle of Carham, '*carrum*', in 1018. By that time the western part of Northumbria had become Cumberland and at the Norman Conquest Yorkshire was fully independent. All these divisions were late by comparison with what happened in the South of England.

Durham appears for the first time in records as Dunholm, 'hill-island', about 1000, and it is obvious that its magnificent site explains its subsequent history as the seat of a martial bishopric. The rock on which it stands is practically surrounded by the river Wear, so enjoyed unique advantages for defensive fortification in days when Scottish raids were to be expected at any time of day or night. Its ecclesiastical importance sprang from the security it gave to the incorrupt and miracle-working body of St Cuthbert, the patron saint of Northumbrians, at a time when Durham was still part of Northumbria. Cuthbert was a shepherd boy from the Lammermoor hills who withdrew from his fellows to live as a hermit on one of the Farne Islands. In 684 he was persuaded to become bishop of Lindisfarne, but he returned to his cell and died there in 687. After Lindisfarne, where he was buried, had been ravaged and laid waste by Norwegians in 793 the saint's remains began a trail of wanderings until they found what was thought to be security in the site of a Roman camp at Chester-le-Street, the Christian metropolis of the North for one hundred and thirteen years. But when Durham was fortified it was seen to be the one place that offered real security. So Durham, the island on the rock, whose name had been given its final form by the Normans, gained two sources of power: the one spiritual, the other martial, and when these were combined under a succession of 'prince-bishops', the result was a form of militant Christianity exercised with regal authority, enforced by bishop's courts, over an area that extended well into the present county of Northumberland. In time of insurrection the Bishop of Durham might even lead his own army against an enemy.

The reason for Durham always having 'County' before its name is historical. When the bishop had land in both counties, his estates in Northumberland were called 'North Durham', and those nearer home 'County Durham'. When the Palatinate jurisdiction of the bishops was abolished in 1836, North Durham was absorbed into Northumberland, but Durham retained its historic designation in preference to adopting a 'shire' terminal.

The power of the bishop in Durham was matched in Northumberland, which was under even greater threat from across the Scottish border, by the creation of the great earldom held for centuries by the Percies. The effect of having these powerful magnates holding sway over a vast region along the Scottish border at the time of the Norman Conquest was that the barons whose arrival had such a revolutionary effect on Yorkshire made little difference to Durham and Northumberland. They built their castles and established such boroughs as Newcastle-upon-Tyne, but when they did so they were not transforming an existing society but merely infiltrating it. Defensive works were as much part of the Northumbrian way of life as they were of the Norman. The defences along the Roman Wall were already supplemented by the great landowners, who built castles of their own at Wark, Etal, Ford, Chillingham, Dunstanborough, Alnwick, Warkworth, Morpeth – 'murderpath' – adequate to withstand short sieges and, in addition to these, there were many pele towers. All along the Wall are places with 'wall' in their name: Wallsend, Walbottle, Heddon-on-the-Wall, and the rest of them.

A characteristic of this social structure was the creation of Liberties, or franchises, each enjoying a high degree of independence. The most influential of these were Durham, Hexham, Tynemouth, North and South Tynedale and Redesdale. As an example of this independence, Wark on Tyne was the head of the Liberty of Tynedale, which was carved out of the Northumberland earldom and held by a line of Scottish kings. When Robert Bruce raided the area in 1314, he made the men of Tynedale do homage to him after Bannockburn. So it is not surprising that the whole of the beautiful landscape of rural Northumberland is covered with place-names reminiscent of both its monastic and martial traditions. Without some knowledge of these they cannot be understood.

The reference Bannockburn, and the knowledge that St Cuthbert started his life on the Lammermoor hills, reduce our surprise in noticing that many Northumberland place-names have a Scottish ring about them, and that the lay-out of many villages, such as Otterburn and Warkworth, is Scottish baronial rather than English. The same goes for minor features in place-names. A stream is neither an English brook nor a Scandinavian beck, but a burn; a small-holding is a shieling. Both Northumberland and Durham before the Industrial Revolution were counties in which there was sharp contrast between the lives of the poor and the lives of the rich. It was like Scotland again in this; and like Scotland both rich and poor were again no less sharply divided between those with a great zeal for learning and religion and those who lived dissolute, devil-may-care lives, defying all conventions. It was characteristic of the North that Durham's twentieth-century new town was not tacked on to an existing place as in the South, but was given the name of a reformed drunkard who became a miners' leader, Peterlee (Peter Lee).

It was in the castles of Northumberland that the Border minstrels sang their ballads, extolling the bravery of the Percies and the lesser nobles, such as the Bruces at Hartlepool, the Baliols at Barnard Castle, the Nevilles at Raby, while the prince-bishop had his castles at Stockton and Auckland as well as at Durham. Of one of the most popular of the ballads sung in these castles, *The Ballad of Chevy Chase*, which recounts the events on a moonlight night in 1388 when the Battle of Otterburn was fought, Sir Philip Sidney wrote that 'it stirred his blood like the sound of a trumpet'. But nobody has evoked the spirit of northern place-names more romantically than Sir Walter Scott in *Rokeby*, as he surveyed the Tees from Barnard Castle:

> Staindrop, who, from her silvan bowers,
> Salutes proud Raby's battled towers:
> The rural brook of Egliston,
> And Balder, named from Odin's son;
> And Greta, to whose banks ere long
> We lead the lovers of the song;
> And silver Lune, from Stainmore wild,
> And fairy Thorsgill's murmuring child,
> And last and least, but loveliest still,
> Romantic Deepdale's slender rill.

So it is fitting that Sir Walter should have the last word in a region in which Scottish influence has always been so strong.

Appendix
A Topographical Glossary

Farmsteads and Villages

A E R N house (Arne, Do.; Crewkerne, Do.; Chard, Do.; Boldre, Ha.), O.E. *aern*.

B A I L, B A I L E Y an outer fortification, or area enclosed by it, O.F.

B A R N barn, also indicating barley, O.E. *berern*.

B A R T O N farmstead; in D. developed to mean demesne farm, or, more commonly, outlying grange, O.E. *beretun*.

B I G G I N building, N. of E., O.Scan, *byggia*.

B O D, B O L D, B O T dwelling house (Bodmin, Co.), Celt. & O.E. *bod, bold, botl*.

B O O S E Y cattle shed, byre (Birley, Db; Birstall, YW.), O.E. *byre*.

B O O T H temporary shelter (Bootham, Y.; Bootle, Cu.; The Booths, Fylde, La.), O.N. & O. Dan. *bóth*.

B O T H Y one-roomed shelter, O.N. *bustadr*.

B U I S T homestead, O.N. & O.Dan.

B U R cottage, dwelling (Bures, Ess., also in names including Bower), O.E. *bur*.

B Y farmstead, village, an element in most Danish names of settlements, O.N. & Dan. *by*.

C O T, C O T E cottage, shelter (Woodmancote, Gl.; N. of E. frequently, and Ascot Brk.), O.E. *cot*.

C U R T A I N court-yard, straw yard, Lat. *cortina*.

G A L I L E E porch devoted to special purposes.

G R A N G E granary farm, frequently preceded by place-name; the place where crops were stored for a feudal lord.

H A M village, manor, homestead, O.E. *ham*.

H A R D W I C K farm for herd of animals, O.E. *heordewic.*

H E L M a shelter (Wo. and commonly in N. of E., where it suggests protection as a helmet), Dan. *hjelm.*

H E W I S H , H U I S H , &c. homestead (Hewish, So.), O.E. *hiwisc.*

L A R T loft, W. of E.

L A T H E barn, N. of E., O.Scan. hlada.

M I S T A L L byre (may be milk-stall).

S C A L E temporary hut (Seascale, Cu.), O.N. *skali.*

S E A L hall, dwelling-house (becomes 'zeal' in Do.), O.E. *sele.*

S E T T L E seat, abode (Settle, YW.), O.E. *setl.*

S H I P P O N cowshed, N. of E., O.E. *scypen.*

S P E N C E pantry (now N. of E. dialect), place from which food and drink are dispensed, O.F. *despense.*

S T A L L place, stall (common everywhere), O.E. *stall.*

T H O R P dependent settlement, less important than a -by, O.Scan.

T O F T homestead (Lowestoft, Sf.), O.N. *toft.*

T O N homestead, village, town, continued in use in place-names until Post Conquest times, O.E. *tún.*

T U F F I L L a lean-to shed, a pent-house.

W E E K , W I C H , W Y K E dwelling-place, hamlet, village, town, often combined with -ham or -comb (Droitwich, Wo., Greenwich, Harwich, Ipswich and many others), O.E. *wic.*

W I C when remaining a farm had come to mean 'dairy farm' by the Norman Conquest.

Farmland

A C R E enclosure or field when found in place-names (Acre, Nf.), O.E. *aecer.*

A K E R L E Y land assigned to the ploughman, *aecer -man.*

A K R plot of cultivated land (Muker, YN.; Stainacre, YN), O.N. *akr.*

A L A G E remote land near parish boundary, M.E. *alange.*

A N G E R grassland (Ongar, Ess.; Angram, La. YN.YW.), O.E. *angr.*

A Y N A M land newly taken into cultivation. N. of E., O.N. *afnám.*

B A L K ridge left unploughed to mark a strip or field boundary, O.E. *balca.*

B A L L field, So.

B A R T H a sheltered pasture for calves (berth?).

B A U L K , B U T T a loft above a barn, N. of E.

B E N T ground covered with coarse grass, O.E. *beonet.*

B I N K S Northern form of balks.

B O V A T E an oxgang or as much land as one ox could plough in a year.

B R A C K land broken up for cultivation, O.N. *brak.*

B R E C K uncultivated land, O.E. *braec.*

C A N G L E fenced enclosure, Ess. & Hrt., M.E. *cangel.*

C A R U C A T E as much land as eight oxen with one plough could till in a year.

C A T C H L A N D unclaimed land, Nf.

C A T C H P O L E strip of land on parish boundary, Nf. & Sf.

C L O S E small enclosure, O.F. *clos*

C L U N , C L Y N E meadow, Welsh *clyn.*

C R O F T small enclosure, corrupted to crap in W. of E., O.E. *croft.*

D E L F , D E L P H quarry, O.E.

D E N a swine pasture, K. and east Sx., O.E. *denn.*

D I L L I C A R a small field, Lake District, O.N.

D O L E a share in a common meadow or field, M.E.

D O O L as 'balk' above, Ess.

E A V E S edge (Bashall Eaves, YW.), M.E.

E R G H shieling, O.N. *erg.*

F I E L D originally unenclosed land, since 14th c. fenced-in land, O.E. *feld.*

F O L D enclosure for animals, O.E. *fald.*

F O S T A L L , F O R E S T A L a paddock or way to front of farmhouse (forestall), K. & Sx.

F O T H E R odd scrap of land in open field, O.E.

G A R S T O N grassy enclosure, paddock, O.E. *gaers-tun.*

G A R T H as 'close' above, cognate with garden, N. of E., O.N.

G R A T T O N stubble field, O.F.

G R E E P trench, M.E. *grepe.*

G R O O P a sheep pen, N. of E.

G W E A L open field, Co.

H E M M E L field, N. of E.

H I D E as measure of ploughed land assessed for taxation.

H I T C H E D L A N D part of common field withdrawn from rotation cultivation.

H O P P I T as 'close' above.

I N G specifically used in agriculture for a common pasture in the N. of E.,
O.N. *eng.*

I N T A K E land taken from the moor, Scan.

L A I N E open field, S. of E.

L A M M A S   L A N D land commonable after haysel.

L A U N D E woodland pasture, O.F. *launde*

L E A S E ,   L E E S ,   L E Y S bears many meanings. Originally a clearing in
a wood, now often used for meadow or pasture land.

L E Y L A N D land in a common field laid down to grass for a period.

L I T T E N burial ground, 'church litten', O.E.

L Y N C H boundary, cognate with links.

L Y N C H E T T cultivated shelf on hillside, O.E. *hlinc.*

M E A R boundary, O.E.

M E A D O W land under grass, O.E.

M E E R as 'balk' above, Gl.

M O O R wasteland, moorland, O.E.

M U D G E mud, D. and Co.

N O D D O N S raised banks on flood plain, Ca.

P A D D O C K ,   P A R R O C K a small field, usually near stable or attached
to stud farm.

P I G H T L E small enclosure or croft, East Ang.

P I N F O L D pound or lock-up

P I N G L E as Pightle, Nt.

P L A S H E T swampy meadow, O.F. *plascq.*

P L A T T level field or simply a plot.

P O U L D E R a reclaimed piece of land, K.

R A I N may be a strip of land on a boundary in places where there is
Dutch influence.

R O Y D a clearing in a forest, common in Y., O.N.

S E A T (s e t t) hill pasture, shieling, N. of E., O.N. *saetre.*

S E L I O N strip of arable land.

S E L L E T a low dairy pasture, O.N.

S L E E T flat meadow, sometimes Sleights in N. of E., O.N. *sletta.*

S M E E D a level piece of ground, M.E. *smethe.*

S N A B a small field enclosed from waste, Dan.

S N A P E a swampy place in a field, occurs in many place-names, especially in the S. of E.

S P O N G a long narrow strip of land.

S T A N G a rood, pole, boundary mark, N. of E., O.N.

STENT boundary, O.F. *estente*.
STITCH a ridge of arable land dividing strips, as balk.
THWAITE a clearing, N. of E., O.N.
TYE an outlying common, Ess. and Sf.
WARPS flat beds of ploughed land, Nf., Dan. *varp*.
WISH a damp meadow, marsh, common in Sx. field names.
WONG a meadow associated with a homestead Le. & Nt. Although
usually given as O.E. it is identical with the O.N. *vangr* in Stavanger.,
O.E. *wang*.
WORTH, WORTHY enclosure round a homestead, O.E.
WRAY nook of land, N. of E., O.N. *vrá*.

Footpaths and Byways

ALLEY passage, narrow street, walk, O.F. *aller*.
ANSTEY narrow footpath, usually uphill, D., Wa.
BAR gate, York.
BORSTALL a winding path on downland, sometimes Burstall.
CARSIE, CAUSEWAY, CAUSEY raised road across marsh, O.F.
caucie.
CHEWAR pathway, Bk.
CUT a near way, shortest means of approach.
DRANGWAY pathway, D.; DRONG, Do.
DRIFT track along which cattle are driven, M.E.
FARROW a wayfaring, a path, O.E.
FOLLY footpath (Colchester, Ess.)
GATE street or road, N. of E.; in S. of E. a gap or opening, Scan., O.E.
geat.
GINNEL alleyway, La. (In Rochdale, Gank).
LADE a path, origin of Ladbrook.
LANE byway, passage, road between hedges.
LOKE path, Nf.
LONE do., N. of E.
RAIKE sheep track, N. of E., Scan.
ROW walk, Chester, Yarmouth. (Rotten Row in Hyde Park is a ride).
SCAR path, YN., usually steep.
SCORE a cut down a declivity (Lowestoft, Sf.).

SLAY lane through gorse, Su.

SNICKET path between gardens.

TRAVERS, TRAVIS a crossing on a road starting from a highway.

TWISS, TWITCH, TWITCHEN a narrow passage connecting streets, La. The origin may be twist or twitch.

VENNEL passage, N. of E.

WANT, WENT, WEINT, WAYLETT place where two or more roads meet or cross. Probably from way or went.

WYND alley, probably a variant of wind.

Hills and Raised Ground

ALT hill, La., Welsh *allt.*

BANK ridge, embankment, N. of E. (Firbank, We.; Bank Newton Y.), O. Dan.

BARROW hill, mound, tumulus. It occurs in Bergholt, Sf. Barge is a Northern form of barrow, O.E. *beorg.*

BOLT headland (Bolt Head D.), O.E.

BRAE hillside, slope, O.N. *brá.*

BRANT, BRENT, BRIND steep land, O.N. *brant.*

BREAST land rounded like a breast.

BRECK hill slope, N. of E. (Norbreck, La.), O.N. *brekka.*

BROW hill slope, N. of E., where it it still pronounced bru. O.E. *bru.*

BUR, BURF hill, tumulus (Buriton, Ha.; Burford, O, Abdon Burf, Sa.), O.E. *beorg.*

BUTT stumpy hill, He. Wa., M.E. *butt.*

CARR stony hill (Cark, La.), Welsh *carreg.*

CLEAVE, CLEEVE, CLIFF steep declivity, O.E. *clif.*

CLINT hill N. of E. (Clint, YN), Dan. *Klint.*

COIGN vantage point, projecting corner.

COPP top, summit (Copp, La.; Copston, Ch.; Orcop, He.), O.E. *copp.*

CRAG steep rock, N. of E. (probably from the Irish *creag* and introduced by the Norwegian Vikings).

CRICK moot hill, rock (Crick, Np.; Crickheath, Sa.; Cricklewood, Mx.), Welsh *creic.*

DOWN (-don) undulating chalk uplands, hill, (Downham, Ca.; Ess., Nf., La), O.E. *dún.*

E D G E ridge, found west of Pennines, O.E. *ecg.*

F E L L hill, mountain, N. of E. (Scawfell, Bow Fell, Cu.), O.N. *feall.*

H A L E nook, corner, recess.

H A U G H mound, N. of E. (Haughton), Scan. *haugr.*

H E A L (- h e a l d) sloping hillside (Yealand, La.; Halstead, Ess.), O.E. *heald.*

H O E tongue of high land, O.E. *hocer.*

H O W E mound, tumulus, YN., O.N. *haugr.*

H U M M O C K mound or hillock.

K N A B steep hill (Nabscar, YN), O.N.

K N A P P top (Knapp, Ha.) In N. of E. often found as Knagg.

K N O C K hillock (Knockin, Sa.), Welsh.

K N O L L a rounded hill (Knole, K.), O.E. *cnoll.*

K N O T T hill (Knott End, La.), O.E. *cnotta.*

L A W , L O W low hill or barrow (Hounslow, Mx.).

L Y T H E slope, YN., O.N.

M O O R waste upland, N. of E., Scan.

M O U N D, M O N T low hill (Mountnessing, Ess.; Mountsorrel, Le.), O.F. & M.E. *mont.*

P E N hill (Pendle, La.), Welsh *penn.*

P I K E pointed hill (Pickhill, YN.; Knocke Pike, We.), O.E. *pic.*

S C O U T peak, N. of E. (Kinder Scout, Db.), O.N. *skúti.*

S L I N D slope (Slinfold, Sx.), O.E.

T O O T look-out hill (Toot Hill, Ess.; Tothill, Ch.), O.E. *totan.*

T O R high rock (Co., D., So., Db. &c.), Welsh & O.E. *tor.*

T U M P hillock, mound or barrow (Hetty Pegler's Tump, Gl.), O.E.

Y I E L D slope, declivity (The Yelde, Db.), O.E. *helde.*

Valleys and Streams

A river, stream (Brathay, La.; Greta, Cu.; Rothay, We.), O.N.

A I T , A Y small island in river (Ayot St Lawrence & Ayot St Peter, Hrt.), O.E. *eg.*

A L N E white river, Wa. & Nb., Brit.

A L T muddy river, La., Brit.

A M B E R water, Db., Brit.

A R K E R winding river, Wa., Brit.

A V O N river (D., Ha., Gl., Le., Np., Wa., Wo., & c.), Welsh *afon*.

A X E river, a variant of Exe.

B A C H E valley of a stream (Wisbech, Ca.; High Beach, Ess.) O.E.

B A Y a dam of pool, Ca.

B E C K brook, N. of E., also from O.E. in Sf. and Li., O.N. *bekkr*.

B O G morass, quagmire, M.E. *bog*.

B O S S fountain, O.E.

B O T T O M a wide shallow valley, suitable for cultivation, La., Ch. border, O.E. *botm*.

B R O O K brook, but in K. and Sx. used for water meadow.

B U M B E Y quagmire, Nf. and Sf.

B U R N stream, bourne in S. is used for an intermittent stream flowing only in winter, O.E.

B Y bend of river (Byfield, Np., Byford, He., not to be confused with Dan. -by), O.E.

B Y H T bend of river (Bitterne, Ha.), O.E.

C A R R marshy land overgrown with brushwood, O.N. *kjarr*.

C A R S E low land along a river, Scan.

C H I N E ravine, Ha., O.E. *cinu*.

C L I N T ravine, N. of E. dialect, also crevice.

C L O U G H narrow valley, N. of E., often pronounced 'clew', O.E. *cloh*.

C L Y S T clean stream, D., related to Clyde, Brit.

C O M B, C O O M B E narrow valley, common in S. of E., also found in Cu. from Welsh *cwm*, O.E. *cumb*.

C R I C K, C R E E K creek, but may mean 'rock' from Welsh *creic*, Brit. *cric*.

C R O N D A L L, C R U N E L a crooked dell, Ha., O.E.

D A L E valley, Y. and Scan. settled districts; but where it occurs in D. Sf. and K. it is derived from O.E. *dael*, O.N. *dalr*.

D E L L a deep hollow or vale (Arundel, Sx.), O.E. *dael*.

D E N E valley, O.E. *denu*.

D I M B L E ravine with water course, Scan.

D I N G L E deep dell (Dingle, La.), M.E. *dingle*.

D O N common river name, not to be confused with the same ending for 'hill', Brit. *dana*.

D O W E L marsh, K.

D U M B L E, D U M P L E land in deep depression, O.E. *dumpel*.

D Y K E trench to carry water, Ca., Li., &c., O.E. *dic*.

E A S E water (Easington, Nb.; Ease Gill), M.E. *yese*.

E M M O T T river confluence, La., O.E. *gemot.*

F E N marshy tract of land (Vange, Ess.; Swinfen, St), O.E. *fenn.*

F I T grassland on river bank, N. of E., O.N. *fit.*

F L A S H water-logged land, swamp, Dan. *flask.*

F L E E T creek, long narrow channel, tidal estuary (Do., Ess., K., Li., Mx.), O.E. *fleot.* O.N., *fijot.*

F O N T spring, well (Bedfont, Mx.), O.E. *funta.*

F O R C E waterfall, N. of E. (High Force, Teesdale), O.N. *foss.*

G I L L ravine, N. of E. (Gaisgill, Scargill, Cowgill), O.N. *gill.*

G O R T whirlpool, weir, O.F.

G O T T channel from a milldam, cognate with gut; in Li. a water drain on the coast, O.N. *grein.*

G O Y T river channel, Ch. Db., Welsh *gwyth.*

G R A I N branch of a valley (Grainsby, Li.) O.N. *grein.*

G R I F F a deep narrow valley, N. of E. (Griffe, Db.), O.N. *gryfia.*

H A L E , H A U G H , H A L G E narrow valley, Ch., Ess., Ha., La., Li., &c., O.E.

H A R D firm ground on bank of river, Ha.

H O P E a blind valley, also dry land in a fen, (Meathorp, We.), O.E. *hop.*

I S C A water, element in Axe, Exe, Usk, Wiske, Brit.

K E L D spring, well, N. of E., common in Scandinavian settled districts (Keldholme, YN), O.N. *kelda.*

K E T T L E round basin, narrow valley (Kettlewell, YN.), Dan. *ketel.*

K I D D L E illegal weir used for fish poaching.

L A T C H , L E A C H stream, bog (Latchford, Ch., O.), O.E. *lache.*

L A V A N T a river name, Sx.; a word used in some districts for a spring breaking out of the downs and dry during the summer, Brit.

L A V E R also a river name, YW., meaning 'babbling brook'. Welsh *llafar*, vocal, resounding, Brit.

L E E T a lead or channel artificially made to carry water (Evenlode, Wo.), O.E. *lád.*

L O D E open drain in fens (Lode, Ca.)

L O O E marsh, pool, inlet of water, Welsh *llwch.*

L U M B deep pool.

M I R E bog, swampy ground, Scan. *myra.*

M O S S morass, YW. (Moston, Ch.), O.N. *mosi.*

O V E R bank of river (Over, Ca.), O.E. *ofer.*

P I L L pool, creek, W. of E., also Pilling, La., Welsh *pyll.*

R A K E , R A I K E S , pass, narrow valley, Su. Sx., O.E. *hraca.*

R H I N E large drain or channel, So. Exmoor, O.E. *rynel*.

R I T H a small stream; becomes rithe or ride in Ha. and Sx. dialect, O.E. *rith*.

S A S S sluice.

S C A R T H a pass (N. of E. in Scandinavianised form), O.E. *sceard*.

S L A C K land in a valley, O.N. *slakki*.

S L A D E valley, O.E. *slaed*.

S T A I T E landing place on bank of river.

S T R A I T narrow passage of water.

S T R A T H a wide valley, Welsh *strat*.

S T R O O D marshy land, found in many place-names, O.E. *strod*.

S Y K E a stream, a trench, Brit. *sic*.

W A T H a ford, N. of E., O.N. *vattr*.

W E Y , W Y E identical river names, *Brit*.

W H A M morass, La. and YW., O.N. *hvammr*.

Woodlands

A C , - O C K oak (Acton, Ch., Gl., He., Mx., Sa., St.), O.E. *ac*.

A L D E R alder (Aldershot, Ha., and in names in Ch. Brk., Nf. &c.). Care is needed to ensure that 'ald' is not for 'old'.

A P P L E apple (Appleby, Cu. and in names in D. Brk., Sx., YN., Ha., Cu., YW., Np., La., too numerous to list).

A S H ash, like the three above is common throughout the country.

These four examples are sufficient to show how common the use of trees was in place-names.

A S S A R T an enclosure of waste after the trees have been grubbed up, O.F.

B A R R O W grove, wood (Bare, Barrowford, La.), O.E. *bearu*.

B E A R , B E E R , B E R E wood, mainly in W. of E.

B O S K thicket, plantation, (Bushey, Hrt.), M.E. *boske*.

B R A K E brushwood, thicket (Brackenborough, Li.; Brackley, Np.,) M.L.G. *brake*.

B R E W E L L , B R O W E L L , B R U E L wood, thicket, hence the 'Broyl of Bedewind' in Savernake, O.F. *breuil*.

B R U S H broom undergrowth, heather.

C L U M P cluster of trees or shrubs, O.E. *clympre*.

COCKSHOTT broad glade through which woodcocks might shoot into nets.

COED wood, Border of Wales and Chetwode, Bk., Welsh.

COPSE, COPPICE underwood grown for periodical cutting, M.E. *copis*.

COVERT thicket hiding game, O.F. *covrir*.

FRITH woodland, usually covert for game (Chapel-en-le-Frith, Db.; Glenfrith, Le.) Fright is a Kentish form of frith, O.E. *fyrhþ*.

GLADE passage between trees, O.E.

GROVE thicket (Grove, Bk.; Graveley, Ca.; Gravesend, K.), O.E. *graef*.

GWITH trees, Co. also GWYTH, (Trengweath, 'village among trees').

HAGG woodland marked for felling, Scan.

HANGER a wood on a hillslope, O.E. *hangra*.

HAYS, HEYS enclosure in forest for preserving game.

HOAD, HOATH heath (Hadley, Hrt.; Hoathley), O.E.

HOLT wood, copse, O.E. *holt*.

HURST woodland clearing, knoll, copse, K. and Sx., O.E. *hyrst*.

KELLY grove, Co. (Kelly, D., Kenley Sr.), Welsh *celli*.

LUND, LOUND a sacred grove (Lund, La., YE., YW., Lound; Nt. Sf.), O.N. *lundr*.

PURLIEU land on edge of forest, M.E. *purley*.

RIDDING, RIDING clearing (Ridding, Db.), O.E. *ryding*.

SCOUGH wood (Myerscough, La.), O.N. *skogr*.

RIPEL strip of wood, coppice (Ripley, Db.), O.E. *ripel*.

ROYD land cleared of trees, N. of E., O.N.

RUPELL a coppice, So.

SCOUGH wood (Myerscough, La.), go.N. *skogr*.

SCROGGS land covered with brushwood, M.E. *scrogge*.

SHAVE copse, K.

SHAW wood or copse, N. of E., but also in Shaw, Brk., and Shawbury, Sa., from O.E. *scaga*, O.N. *sceage*.

SKEW wood (Skewsby, YN.; Aiskew, YN.), O.N. *skógr*.

STORTH brushwood (Storrs, La.; Storth, We.), O.N. *storth*.

TALLIS copse.

WALD, WALT, WEALD, WOLD woodland (care to be taken to ensure that names prefixed by Wald or Walt are not indicating Welsh or British settlements). Wold in the Cotswolds and the Yorkshire Wolds means open upland, O.E. *wald*.

WITH, WYTHE woodland (Tockwith; Askwith YW.), Scan *vithr*.

List of abbreviations used in the Glossary

County and Racial Abbreviations

Bd. Bedfordshire
Bk. Buckinghamshire
Brk. Berkshire
Ca. Cambridgeshire
Ch. Cheshire
Co. Cornwall
Cu. Cumberland
D. Devon
Db. Derbyshire
Do. Dorset
Du. Durham
Ess. Essex
Gl. Gloucestershire
Ha. Hampshire
He. Herefordshire
Hrt. Hertfordshire
Hu. Huntingdonshire
K. Kent
La. Lancashire
Le. Leicestershire
Li. Lincolnshire
Mx. Middlesex
N. of E. North of England
Nb. Northumberland
Nf. Norfolk
Np. Northamptonshire

Nt. Nottinghamshire
O. Oxfordshire
O.Dan. Old Danish
O.E. Old English
O.F. Old French
O.N. Old Norse
R. River name
Ru. Rutland
Sa. Shropshire
Scand. Scandinavian
Sf. Suffolk
So. Somerset
Sr. Surrey
St. Staffordshire
Sx. Sussex
W. Wiltshire
Wa. Warwickshire
We. Westmorland
Wo. Worcestershire
Y. Yorkshire
YE. East Riding, or East York-
shire
YN. North Riding or North York-
shire
YW. West Riding or West York-
shire

Bibliography

Anderson, O.S., *The English Hundred Names* (three vols.) Lund, 1934–36.

Blair, J. Hunter, *An Introduction to Anglo-Saxon England*, Camb., 1936.

Bradley, H. *Collected Papers*, Oxford, 1928.

Beckinsale, R. P., *Anglo-Saxon England to AD 1420*, Oxford.

Camden, W., *Remains Concerning Britain, 1605*, reprinted E. P. Pubs., 1974.

Cameron, K., *English Place Names*, 2nd ed., Batsford, 1977.

Chadwick, H. M., *The Origin of the English Nation*, Camb., 1907.

Chadwick, N. K. (editor) *Celtic Britain*, London, 1963.

Collingwood, W. G., *The Angles in Furness and Chartmel, Trans. of the Cumb. & West. Antiq. & Arch. Soc.*, vol. xxiv, 1924.

Collingwood, W. G., *Lake District History*, Kendal, 1925.

Collingwood, R. G. and Myers, J. N. L., *Roman Britain and the English Settlements*, 2nd ed., Oxford, 1956.

Copley, C. J., *English Place Names and Their Origins*, Exeter, 1971.

Cox, R. Hippesley, *The Green Roads of England*, London, 1914.

Darby, H. C., *An Historical Geography of England before AD 1800*, Cam., 1936.

Dickins, Bruce, *English Names and Old English Heathenism, Essays and Studies by Members of the English Assn.*, vol. xix, 1933.

Ekwall, E., *The Concise Oxford Dictionary of English Place-Names*, Oxford, 1966.

Ekwall, E., *English River-Names*, Oxford, 1928.

Ekwall, E., *The Place-Names of Lancashire*, Manchester, 1922.

Ekwall, E., *Scandinavians and Celts in the North-West of England*, Lund, 1918.

Field, J., *English Field-Names*, Exeter, 1972.

Fox, C., *The Personality of Britain*, London, 1943.

Gelling, M., Nicolaisen, W. F. H., and Richards, M., *The Names of Towns and Cities in Britain*, Batsford, 1970.

Hoskins, W. G., *The Making of the English Landscape*, London, 1955.

Hoskins, W. G., *Provincial England*, London, 1963.

Kemble, J. M., *The Saxons in England*, London, 1849.

Leonard, R., *Rural England, 1086–1135*, London, 1959.

Loyn, H. R., *Anglo-Saxon England and the Norman Conquest*, London, 1962.

McClure, E., *British Place-Names in their Historical Setting*, E. P. Pubs., 1972 (reprint).

Margary, J. D., *Roman Roads in Britain* (3rd ed.) London, 1973.

Mawer, A., *Problems of Place-Name Study*, Camb., 1929.

Myers, J. N. L., Article in *Antiquity*, 1935.

Oman, C. W., *England Before the Norman Conquest* (revised ed.), 1937.

Reaney, P. H., *The Origin of English Place-Names*, London, 1960.

Smith, A. H., *English Place-Name Elements*, 2 vols. Camb., 1956.

Smith, A. H., *Place-Names and the Anglo-Saxon Settlement*, Proc. of the Brit. Academy, Camb., 1956.

Stenton, F. M., *English Feudalism*, Oxford, 1932.

Stenton, F. M., *Anglo-Saxon England*, 2nd ed. Oxford, 1947.

Stenton, F. M., *The Historical Bearing of Place-Name Studies*, Trans. of the Royal Hist. Soc., 4th Series, vols. xxi-xxvi, 1939–45.

Stenton, F. M., *The Danes in England*, Oxford, 1957.

Taylor, I., *Names and their Histories*, London, 1896.

Wainwright, F. T., *Archaeology and Place-Names and History*, London, 1962.

Whitelock, D., *The Beginnings of English Society: The Anglo-Saxon Period*, London, 1952.

Zachrisson, R. E., *Anglo-Norman Influence in English Place-Names*, Lund, 1909.

The Publications of the English Place-Name Society, The Making of the English Landscape Series (edited by W. G. Hoskins), and Regions of the British Isles Series (edited by W. Gordon East).

Index

149